The Essential Wisdom and Lore from a Lifetime of Salmon Fishing

DECORATIONS BY PAUL BACON

SIMON & SCHUSTER

NEW YORK   LONDON   TORONTO   SYDNEY   TOKYO   SINGAPORE

Salmon on a Fly

Lee Wulff

edited by
John Merwin

SIMON & SCHUSTER
Simon & Schuster Building
Rockefeller Center
1230 Avenue of the Americas
New York, New York 10020

Copyright © 1992 by The Estate of Lee Wulff
Introductions copyright © 1992 by John Merwin

Designed by Theresa Cassaboon

Manufactured in the United States of America

10   9   8   7   6   5   4   3   2   1

Library of Congress Cataloging-in-Publication Data
Wulff, Lee.
    Salmon on a fly : the essential wisdom and lore from
  a lifetime of salmon fishing / Lee Wulff ; edited by John
  Merwin.
        p.   cm.
    Includes index.
    1. Salmon fishing. 2. Fly fishing. I. Merwin,
  John.   II. Title.
SH684.W85   1992
799.1'755—dc20   91-40845   CIP
ISBN 0-671-76065-3

*Grateful acknowledgment is made to the following periodicals,
where portions of this book previously appeared:*

"Ability to Woo Fish and Anglers Alike" © 1991 by The
New York Times Company, reprinted by permission: Fore-
word by Nelson Bryant. *The Anglers' Club* [NY] *Bulletin*:
Chapter 28. *The Atlantic Salmon Journal*: Chapters 8–9, 11–
12, 14–19, 21–23, 26–27, 30. *Country Life*: Chapter 3. *Field
& Stream*: Chapters 5–7. *Fly Fisherman*: Chapter 24. *Fly Rod
& Reel*: Chapters 28–29. *Garcia Fishing Annual*: Chapter 13.
Outdoor Life: Chapter 10. *Sports Afield*: Chapter 20. *The Spur*:
Chapters 2, 4. *Trout*: Chapter 25.

CONTENTS

Contents

Contents

FOREWORD

Lee Wulff was possessed by a furious desire to refine the art of angling and was extraordinarily successful in that quest, right to the end of his eighty-six years.

The refinements were not only in technique and tackle; a half century or so ago, he became the first major exponent of the catch-and-release philosophy. He helped to persuade subsequent legions of anglers that wooing, playing and ultimately releasing a splendid gamefish was often more pleasurable than killing it, that such fish are too valuable to be caught only once.

Wulff was anticipating the time when angling pressure would decimate stocks of wild species, among them trout. It is fitting that close by the hillside home in the Catskills where he and his wife, Joan, lived, there are no-kill stretches of the Willowemoc and Beaverkill rivers where one fishes for fun rather than to fill one's creel, where all trout must be set free.

Wulff also battled unrelentingly to protect the Atlantic salmon—perhaps the world's most highly prized game and food fish—from overexploitation.

At the meetings of the Atlantic Salmon Federation, a Canadian–American conservation organization, Wulff, who was a federation director and officer, often reiterated his conviction that there should be no commercial harvesting of wild Atlantic salmon.

Wulff's enormous prestige was a major factor in the success of the federation's membership drive in Quebec and New Brunswick in the early 1980s. He and Joan visited those provinces, convincing salmon fishermen that the federation's efforts on behalf of the species were worthwhile.

Although he was often dogmatic and unbending and had no fear of treading on anyone's toes, most of those whom Wulff encountered soon understood that his fundamental concern was for the salmon, that he had no other ax to grind. He was the conscience of the Atlantic salmon restoration effort in North America.

"No one," said Joseph Cullman III, chairman of the federation in the United States, "has contributed as much to the salmon conservation movement as Lee Wulff."

Meeting in Manhattan a few days after Wulff died April 28, 1991, in the crash of a private plane he was flying, the United States branch of the federation approved a resolution supporting a total ban on all commercial fishing for wild Atlantic salmon.

(Such a goal is not farfetched when one realizes that of the 235,000 metric tons of Atlantic salmon sold throughout the world in 1990, only 10,000 metric tons were wild fish. The remainder came from salmon farms.)

Although an accomplished big-game fisherman—he pioneered rod-and-reel fishing for giant bluefin tuna off Newfoundland and twice, in the waters of that province, set world records for the species—Wulff is better known as a fly fisherman.

He was among the first to take bonefish on a fly, and in 1967 off Salinas, Ecuador, he caught a 148-pound striped marlin on a five-ounce fly rod and a reel without a drag. That fish remains the fly-rod record for the species on twelve-pound-test tippet. Earlier this year, he became the first, off Costa Rica, to take a sailfish on a dry fly.

The short fishing vests that nearly all fly fishermen now wear when wading were created by Wulff, as were the hair wing Wulff series of dry flies without which a trout or salmon angler would feel ill-equipped.

Always an advocate of using the lightest tackle possible, Wulff was probably the one most responsible for persuading American anglers that smaller, shorter, one-handed fly rods rather than the huge two-handed outfits favored in the United Kingdom were the tools with which to pursue Atlantic salmon.

Wulff's enthusiasm for life and angling never seemed to wane. In 1985, looking for new challenges, he decided to try to catch an Atlantic salmon on a tiny, #28 dry fly. No one had done that before. The hook for such a fly is less than one-eighth of an inch long. I was with the Wulffs on New Brunswick's Upsalquitch River when he launched that effort. He went forth and hooked a salmon but it broke off when the fragile leader rubbed against a rock. A few days later on the nearby Restigouche, he hooked and landed a ten-pounder on another #28.

Two years ago when we were together on the Ste. Marguerite River in Quebec, Lee was still at it, trying to better his #28 record.

It was a dark, cold, wet day. Lee hooked a salmon of fifteen pounds or more and I stood beside him as he played it, helping him move—he had a bad ankle—along the black, slippery rocks as he followed the fish down the pool. After a run of about seventy-five yards, the fish sulked.

Streaming with rain, Lee's craggy face was a study in rapt concentration. Holding the line between the thumb and forefinger of his reel hand with consummate delicacy, he half whispered to me:

"When you have caught enough of these fish, you can feel their heartbeats, can tell what they are going to do next. And this one is about to depart."

The fish departed on another run and twenty minutes later the hook pulled loose. I am sure that he did feel the salmon's heartbeat. I am also sure that Lee Wulff's own heartbeat—his restless search for new angling frontiers, his fierce integrity, his concern for the natural world's well-being—will be felt by those who take rod in hand a century hence.

—Nelson Bryant

Introduction

From tackle and tactics through fly patterns and casting, Lee Wulff has been the most influential fly fisherman of our time. He dramatically changed the way many people think about conservation of fishery resources and dramatically changed the way fishermen think about their fishing. This applies to all kinds of fishing, from trout to giant tuna and marlin. But nowhere have his contributions been more evident than in the world of Atlantic salmon.

Wulff probably spent more time fighting for Atlantic salmon conservation than he spent actually fighting the fish on the end of a line, and his activity in both areas spanned more than sixty years. He recorded much of both in a series of magazine articles over the same period, many of which appear here for the first time in book form. Ranging from the 1930s through the 1990s, the experiences and salmon savvy in these pages are all vintage Wulff and all immensely helpful to salmon anglers everywhere.

We've arranged this book's chapters chronologically, for the most part, because as such they are historical documents that reflect the development of both salmon angling in general and its foremost exponent. In early chapters, for example, you'll see reference to Lee's use of traditional double-hooked salmon flies. In later chapters, you'll see him condemning their use because he finally decided they were simply unfair to the fish and didn't really work better than single-hooked flies anyway. As a means of keeping such changes in context, I've added a short introduction to each chapter.

Atlantic-salmon fishing these days is a growing sport. Some rivers in both North America and Europe whose salmon populations were decimated in years past by dams, pollution and overfishing are starting to recover. A growing conservation ethic surrounding salmon is the reason, and that's a gospel Lee Wulff preached long and hard since the 1930s. The fight isn't over by any means, and I call your particular attention to Chapter 26, in which Wulff argues persuasively that salmon need and deserve the protection that could be afforded by their legal designation as gamefish in Canada and elsewhere.

Having helped to restore the salmon runs and while working to preserve them, Wulff will also show you how to catch salmon. His salmon-fishing experience is without peer, which makes all the instruction and advice in these pages both credible and valuable. As the late Arnold Gingrich once wrote, "As far back as 1939, Lee Wulff has been the answer man if you wanted some new dodge or wrinkle that would make your fishing easier, simpler, handier or more efficient...." Simply put, this book will make you a better salmon fisherman.

Wulff and I finished working on this manuscript in early April 1991, and celebrated over dinner at the Antrim Lodge near his home on the Beaverkill. Two weeks later he was dead, *Salmon on a Fly* suddenly became his last book, and I somberly went about changing verb tenses in the various introductions. His influence on the angling world is indelible, just as it was on my own life through our long friendship. It's hard to say good-bye.

JOHN MERWIN
DORSET, VERMONT
APRIL 1991

CHAPTER ONE

THE ATLANTIC SALMON

*I*f you ask a hundred fishermen for their votes on a perfect gamefish, you'll get dozens of different answers, including large- or smallmouth bass, walleyes, bonefish, tarpon, permit, muskellunge, brown trout—and Atlantic salmon. The latter fish is unique in having been characterized as the king among game-fishes since Walton's time. Here are Lee Wulff's thoughts on that recognition, expressed by a man who fished and fought on behalf of salmon for almost six decades.

AS THE GOD OF ANGLING was finishing his task he paused and thought, "Now I will create a superb gamefish, sportier than all the others. Then I will rest."

He mused on, "I will need a fish that goes to sea to season him for distance swimming and endurance. My strongest and fastest swimmers are the pelagic fish of the sea that swim great distances and are slow to tire. I will put him in the northern seas where the colder water will stimulate him and give him the strength and courage that comes from the north temperate zones. He will have a strong, stiff body like the mackerel, the marlin and the tuna with a strong tail that won't bend under a hard stroke like the tails of trout and of cod.

"To bring him within reach of individual anglers I will have to make him anadromous so that he will enter the streams where the lifeblood of the land flows clean and clear as in the beautiful northern trout streams. I will make him like the trout, my best fish yet, but different and better. He will take even smaller flies in proportion to his size, and he will leap higher than any trout ever.

"I will make him of a size that a lone angler can challenge him with light tackle and carry him if he's lucky enough to bag one. In fact, I will make him return to the rivers in varying sizes to give anglers varying challenges and to give him a security in case of a wipeout in river or sea of any single annual crop.

"He will feed ravenously in the sea where the anglers cannot reach him and will come into the rivers of his nativity super-charged with energy for an extended period. I will take away his hunger for I cannot let him eat the trout or his own young that will be sharing the streams with him.

"I will make him dark blue on the back to match the looked-down-on color of the sea when he is in the ocean. He'll have sides and belly of brightest silver so that he'll disappear into the shining surface of the sea when predators from below look up to seek him.

"He will not be knowledgeable of the wiles of anglers if he is away at sea for all that time so I must make him wary of them.

"No. That will not be necessary. If I take away his hunger he will have no urge to take a fly.

"How, then, will I let the anglers catch him?"

He paused and thought.

"I will put certain instincts into his subconscious that will remind him of his youth in the streams where he fed ravenously on the insects of the streams. But I will hide them well, and only on rare occasions will events trigger him to chase or catch a fly. This may be confusing to anglers and to this fish, too, since he himself will not be conscious in advance of the particular fly or movement that will tempt him. He will torment anglers and he will be tormented himself, sometimes to the point of being indecisive right up until the fly is within his bite and then he'll refuse it. He will play with a floating fly—pushing it up with his nose on occasions and changing his mind just a millisecond before he is ready to take it.

"He will have to be brave enough to venture into the shallow waters where there will be safety and food for the progeny of his spawning. And wary enough and swift enough to escape most of the time from the fish hawks and eagles, the eels and otters and all the other predators of the streams and sea. And, yet, I cannot have him fearful enough to hide in brush piles and the like, for then he'd break away from the anglers far too often. Perhaps his long sea sojourn can be made to instill in him a need for open water in which to maneuver so that he will shun the hiding places the trout so often use to escape an angler. That will cause him to make long runs and, of course, he'll leap dramatically to escape the angler's tackle, having long practiced leaping for the falls and rapids he must jump or climb.

"He'll be my masterpiece among all sporting fish, this Atlantic salmon of mine. I hope the anglers of the world will love him above all others, cherish him and challenge him but never forsake him, using all their powers to save him from any and all other predators in sea and stream and to keep his spawning rivers ever bright and clean."

[1990]

CHAPTER TWO

SOMETHING FISHY ABOUT SALMON

Wulff once told me he spent a number of seasons fishing for salmon before starting to write about them, and that experience is evident in this chapter, which was one of his earliest salmon pieces. It originally appeared in a 1937 copy of The Spur, and it already shows a depth of experience that other angling writers should have envied if not emulated.

It's worth noting Wulff's comments in this chapter on the difference between luck and skill in salmon angling, which is a topic that eventually occupies any studious angler. It has appeared often in Wulff's writing, most recently in Chapter 29 of this book, which he wrote more than fifty years after writing this one.

IT WAS NEAR the end of July in Nova Scotia. There had been an unusually long spell of dry weather. All during the month not one salmon had been killed. The club that leased the water allowed none but its members to fish, with the exception of a few small boys who flashed their flies about in the shallow water and amused the older men. Three salmon had taken up a position under the bridge that crossed the river at the lodge. They were in plain view, moving their fins and fanning their tails from time to time in order to keep their positions in the slow current. Club members knew these salmon well enough to call them by their first names, having cast over them with every type of fly in the club's possession. As their habitat was right near the lodge, someone was always fishing for them.

One day the oldest of the kids, a lad of seven named Blair, went home and caught one of his father's geese. Pulling out some white feathers and using some string and a codfish hook, he fashioned an enormous fly. He tied this fly to the end of some white cod line dangling from a rock-maple pole and came back down to the bridge. While two of the club members stood by, smiling, he splashed this fly like a white swallow down on the water near the three fish. And . . . one of them rose, was hooked and dragged ashore in a lather of white water.

A club member immediately bought the fly from Blair for a dollar either in the hope of catching a fish with it himself or else to keep the youngster from catching another. Blair, the enterprising youth, was back in an hour with a similar creation, but neither he nor the club member ever caught another salmon on those flies.

Which all goes to show that the Atlantic salmon is a strange breed. The first two to five years of his life are spent in freshwater streams, and during those years we know pretty much what he does and why. He grows up in about the same way as a young trout does under similar conditions. Then, suddenly, one day in spring he puts on a coat of silver and rushes out to the ocean, a proceeding which mystifies us a great deal. The young salmon, or parr, may change to his silver coat at the age of two years, three years, four years or even five years. This difference in the amount of time spent in fresh water is another thing we have a hard time explaining.

When the young salmon gets his silver coat he is called a smolt and is about six inches long. When he returns from the sea, from one to four years later, he has grown large—and different. The length of time he stays in the ocean determines his growth, and we wonder why some stay only one year before spawning while others stay four years and grow about four times as big. Where they have been all this time keeps us guessing.

When the salmon comes back to his native stream, or sometimes to another river, for the purpose of spawning he no longer relies on the food coming down in the stream for subsistence. He just doesn't eat—but may rise to an occasional nymph or insect. If he did feed like other fish, the streams would soon be skinned of everything edible up to two- or three-pound trout. The mature salmon in that case would eat all the parr he could catch and thus help destroy his own line of succession.

Because he doesn't take much nourishment, a salmon loses from a third to half his weight during his spawning stay—which lasts from four months to a year. Entering the stream from the ocean, the salmon is one of the most beautiful of fish—sleek, silvery and well rounded; he leaves the stream as a kelt, or slink, an ugly, black, large-headed skeleton. He returns to the ocean ravenously hungry to build up his strength and store in his body the energy necessary for another spawning journey.

The fact that a salmon will rise only on a whim and not for the sake of feeding makes this fishing something different. The smallest of lures is sometimes required. I once caught a salmon on a #16 dry fly, a representation of a gnat tied on a hook a quarter of an inch long and an eighth of an inch across, using a leader not much thicker than a human hair and breaking at less than two pounds pull. All the larger flies on heavier leaders had been refused. A native Nova Scotian fishing near me observed, "They love those little flies of yourn, don't they?" while he waggled his head in wonder. All of us who fish for salmon have waggled our heads in wonder at the strangeness of the fish.

A salmon couldn't live on tiny things like those gnats if he tried to. This business is probably only a game with him, a throwback to his baby days in the stream. One fish will take the fly with a savage rush, sinking the hook deep in his throat, while the next one may chase it time after time, swirling behind it yet never touching it. It is quite a different story when he really feeds out in the ocean. There he is possessed with a savage hunger. Salmon netted in salt water have spewed forth three or four full-size herring, just a small part of the day's feeding.

Locating the right time and place to fish for salmon is just about as difficult as getting them to rise. The most successful of the salmon fishing gentry have scouts on the rivers they wish to fish so they can drop everything and rush right up there the minute a big run of fish enters a river. Of course not everyone can do this. Most of us have to plan our trips far in advance. Deciding where to go is tricky business because the river that had the best run last year may not have anything but a few stragglers this season. Or the run that usually arrives late in June may come in this year during the first week of June, instead, or the second week in July. While last year's "best" river may be having punk fishing, some little river that hadn't had a decent run in years might have such a run of fish as to impress even the old-timers.

Hooking a salmon usually requires a certain amount of angling skill. Over a period of time the element of luck straightens itself out—but, Lord knows, it may be an awfully long period. For days on end, even whole seasons, conditions have been such that skillful anglers with the finest equipment were outfished by the dubs with their clumsy tackle and awkward casting. Just talk to some of the men who were up on the Margaree last year [1936]. Salmon fishing is a good sport for the novice to take a fling at— if he catches some salmon he'll have a good time, and if he doesn't he'll find a lot of seasoned casters who haven't had too much luck either.

Salmon in the spawning streams don't lie in wait for food as other fish do. Instead they lie where they are comfortable and safe, moving gradually up toward the spawning beds. A restless energy seems to fill them, causing them to leap out into the air periodically or scoot along just under the surface of the water. In cold, swift currents the salmon may lie motionless for long periods of time, but when in slack water they are almost always active.

Experience gives a man a certain knowledge of the positions salmon will take up in the streams, but it is always a source of satisfaction to know that there really is a salmon out there and that the fly is not passing over blank water. Quite often I have found men casting away over a stretch of river that had no salmon in it at the time. One such man I took to a high place on the bank from which the whole floor of the pool was visible. From that point of vantage it was easy to see that there wasn't a fish in the pool. Instead of being grateful for my keeping him from wasting any more time there, he was exceedingly upset because I had spoiled his fishing.

Knowing the salmon's tendency to keep moving, I usually watch for signs of movement when the water is not clear enough to see the fish. One day, from a high rock overlooking a deep, narrow gorge, I sat waiting for the leap of a salmon. The Little River of Cape Breton has dark brown water discolored by the drainings from the spruce ponds at the edge of the barrens. A salmon in that water drops out of sight when he submerges more than five feet below the surface. This particular pool was small and deep. Water slid in sharply at the head and poured slowly out over a three-foot drop and went racing down through a hundred yards of gorge.

At the tail of this pocket pool a large boulder rose up to block the flow of the stream. It forced the water to either side. On the left, looking downstream, the water poured over a three-foot falls; on the right it seemed to eddy past a pile of rocks and swing back into the body of the pool.

I noticed those things as I waited. I saw, too, that I would never be able to land a fish in that little bit of deep water between the rocks because I couldn't get down to the water's edge on my side of the stream. The rock face of the pool was too sheer below me. But if I were to hook a fish, I reasoned, and he were to go over the falls, I might be able to follow him down through the gorge to the big stillwater where the chance of landing him would be better.

While I sat there considering the landing of a fish (if I were to hook one), I saw two salmon come down out of the black water and make a tour of the pool. The lower section was shallow enough so that I could see the bottom. The salmon came down on the far side, turned across the tail of the pool just above the big boulder, and came up near the shore to pass directly under my overhanging rock. Before they vanished again in the deep, upper water I had an excellent view of them both. One of them was the largest salmon I have ever seen. The other one was a fish of about fourteen pounds, but beside that giant he looked more like a trout than another salmon. I called to my companion who was fishing the pool just above me. He came down and together we watched and waited. At regular intervals those two salmon made the circuit of the pool. Each time they appeared we tried to tempt them with our flies, but they swam lazily on around, taking no notice of our lures.

After an hour my companion grew weary of this one-sided play and returned to his upper pool. After two hours, when I too was ready to give up, the big one rose. I was dapping my fly on the surface of the water almost directly below me on the big fellow's course of travel. He rose lazily, letting his broad back break the surface in the manner of a porpoise, and went down with the fly. When he felt the hook he started ponderously for the far corner of the pool. Not for the spot where the water was pouring out, but toward the back eddy and the pile of rocks. I watched him move unhurriedly toward that mess of ragged stone. The fish and the bottom below him were plainly visible. The strain I put on the line seemed to pass unnoticed by the great fish. He approached the shadow of the rock pile. I waited for him to turn—to come back into deep water—to cross over and go down over the falls. But he simply disappeared. My casting line was almost entirely off the reel before I realized what had happened.

Holding my line solidly, I let the strain exerted by the fish break my leader. I broke the line, knowing that I had no chance of landing that salmon. I realized that there was an opening in the rocks through which water flowed out of the pool, as well as over the falls, and that my fifty-odd pounds of record fish had chosen that exit and gone coursing down the white water toward the still water, pulling my line through the hole after him.

I reeled in my line, crossed the river up above and came down the other shore to investigate. I found the place where the water flowed out through the rocks. It was a much easier way in or out of the pool than the falls provided and a much safer one for the salmon. The amazing thing was that the salmon, a fish fresh from the sea and its limitless space, a fish that by nature shuns narrow confines and shallow water, headed without hesitation for a hole in the rocks so small that he must have scraped his sides as he passed through. So passed my chance for a record salmon.

Salmon don't depend on hiding for safety. They don't dash off wildly, like a trout, at a suspicious movement on the shore. They rely, instead, on their speed to outdistance pursuit. Often a man can approach to within a few feet of them, so long as he does not come between them and the deep, open water they are counting on for safety. They may make no sign that they have seen the angler, not the slightest movement of a fin, yet fishing over them may be futile. On the other hand, sometimes, when other fish would be frightened beyond all consideration of anything but safety, salmon will show a sudden curiosity. Witness an event that occurred on the Dennys River in Maine last July [1937].

With two companions I was casting over a snag-strewn pool in the meadow. It was late afternoon, and we had been fishing steadily and unsuccessfully since early morning. One solitary salmon leaped periodically at a certain spot in the pool. One of my companions was casting to the leaping fish and had been, on and off, for about four hours. The other one was across the stream and above him; I was across the stream and a little below him. I was doing my casting from the top of a bunch of logs that had been piled on the bank by the spring floods. From that point I hooked a chub, a small nuisance of a fish generally considered unfit to eat. Salmon, when they do rise, often take the same tiny insects upon which the small fish feed. So these chub, as well as small trout and parr, are likely to take a fly just in time to prevent a salmon's getting it.

Confronted with this chub, for some unknown reason I was possessed with a wild desire to throw it at the fisherman who was seriously casting for the leaping salmon. Three of us fishing so steadily and determinedly without a word of conversation and without any results offered too good a chance to pass up. I pictured the six-inch chub landing with a startling splash at the feet of the engrossed angler. The chub somehow slipped from my hand as I threw it, and instead of reaching the far bank it fell with a splash in the precise spot where the salmon had been leaping.

If I have ever been embarrassed—that was the time. The water a man fishes in is sacred. His prospective fish is his for as long as he cares to cast. But, upset as I was at the slip of the chub, it was nothing to what came over the object of my throw.

"Good God, man, don't ever, ever do that! You might as well stone the pool," he shouted, and went on to utter a series of not-so-nice things about me. When he finally ran out of words he picked up a long, stripped sapling that was lying on the shore and, wading out, thwacked it down on the water he had been fishing. He twisted it in the current and worked it back and forth like a giant toothbrush. Tiring of that, he let the sapling float off downstream while he clambered up the bank to return with a log that he dumped from his shoulder into the sacred spot I had just despoiled. As a final gesture he resorted to throwing rocks of all sizes into the pool.

My other companion and I, still shaking with laughter, reeled in our lines. Wordlessly the three of us walked upstream to the next pool to try our luck there. Arriving there, we found that two men were already fishing it. The shadows were piling up on the far bank, so we decided to call it a day. Accordingly we turned back.

On passing the pool that had been so effectively stoned, we were surprised to see the same old salmon jumping in the same old spot. My brooding, mistreated friend stripped off some line and, casting out, hooked the fish—our only salmon of the day. It was less than twenty minutes since he had thrown the last stone. Which goes to show that a disturbance that would have ruined fishing for any other kind of fish was just what was needed to make that salmon rise.

A great many salmon fishermen believe that a salmon merely crushes an insect in his jaws, swallowing the juice and ejecting the carcass. In contradiction, I offer this: A friend of mine was fishing with a man who put his rod down and let his fly sink to the bottom while lighting his pipe. A high wind was blowing and it took several matches before he could get the pipe lit. My friend noticed that the man's line was moving in the pool. He shouted, and the fisherman brought his rod up sharply to find himself hooked to a salmon. When the fish was landed it was necessary to cut him open in order to loosen the big Black Dose that was hooked in the side of his stomach. The fish had picked the fly up off the bottom and had actually swallowed it.

Salmon have been landed with the line running into their mouths and out through their gills to the fly caught in their sides. In such a case the fish had taken the fly and expelled it with the water passing through his gills. This falls in with the contention of those who say that a salmon will hang on to anything it takes for at least half a minute. For the opposing group, those who believe that a salmon should be struck immediately when he takes the fly, I offer the fact that once on the Margaree I watched a salmon take my fly and spit it out again before I could set the hook. It seems that nobody has been able to lay down a set of rules that the salmon will even remotely live up to.

There are men who "spot fish" for salmon. They locate rocks or hollows in the stream bed where the salmon should be lying and then pepper these spots with a series of casts. This is generally an effective method. The theory behind it is that the salmon prefer to rise to a fly in a certain spot in their field of vision. Fish have been known to be unmoved by flies passing over anywhere except in one spot. Whenever the fly passed that spot the fish would swirl at the fly and in many cases eventually take it.

In Newfoundland I knew an angler who always dropped his fly just ahead of the salmon and let it swing away in the current. He used no other method, but he was one of the most successful fishermen in that district. One day I watched him cast over a fish for almost an hour, always dropping his fly in that precise spot a few inches in front of the salmon's nose. He was a terribly cocky fellow who was quite upset when, after he'd given the fish up, he saw the same salmon rush a full fifteen feet to take another man's fly.

Salmon are crazy fish, and once they get into a man's blood he's never quite the same. Men so touched will spend long hours looking at salmon scales through microscopes, determining how much time the fish has spent in salt water and how many times he has spawned. They'll go around muttering to themselves about "greased" lines and "double spey" casts. They'll hang over the railings of rickety bridges watching a salmon idly resting in the current or wait there for hours in the hope of seeing one flash by. They'll devote every free minute to getting the right sort of new gadget with which to catch salmon or finding out where the best run will be next year and the exact date. Or they'll tell you that there's no fish like the salmon. On and on they rave about this paragon of all fish, this leaping *Salmo salar,* whose capture is the crowning sporting feat of them all . . . and maybe they're right.

[1937]

CHAPTER THREE

WELL-REMEMBERED SALMON

*T*his chapter also first appeared in 1937 (in Country Life) and introduces a couple of important characters. The first is Nova Scotia's Margaree River, which was a popular stop for American anglers during the years before and after the Second World War. In recent years, that province was the first to restrict the taking of large salmon as a conservation measure. The Margaree is still famous for its fall run of large salmon, so much so that in recent years the river has become increasingly crowded. My latest information is that the province may abandon its long-standing policy of not requiring nonresident anglers to hire a guide and may soon introduce a mandatory guiding system to both alleviate crowding and to provide a boost for the local economy.

The second character is Victor Coty, with whom Wulff got started making films in the 1930s. Coty was a filmmaker and lecturer, and initially Wulff was the "fisherman" in Coty's movies. Eventually, of course, Wulff started filming on his own, which led finally to several years of sports filming for CBS and ABC television and numerous national awards for Wulff as a film producer.

ONE OF THE THINGS a fisherman seldom forgets is his first Atlantic salmon. I feel that I was particularly fortunate in the events and setting surrounding my own first salmon. It was late summer and the scent of hay from the fields of Duncan MacDonald hung heavily in the air. The sunshine that morning was bright, bringing a welcome warmth after the chill of the early dawn. The rose-tinted rocks that make up the graveled bed of the Margaree sparkled as the light wavered down to them through the crystal water. The lower reaches of the Hut pool were glassy in their stillness except for an occasional dimple as a sea trout rose to an insect or a school of young gaspereau leapt clear of the water like a shower of silver darts in the path of a marauder. There was sheer beauty everywhere I looked on that bright summer morning.

My first two days on the river had been blank except for one fish that rose to my fly but was not hooked. That morning, after an hour of steady casting, my sense of expectancy was somewhat dulled. I was casting for the rhythm of casting, for the beauty of seeing the line straighten out and the fly settle down on the dark, dancing water at the head of the pool. It was at the head of the pool where the water is dark and deep and swift as it sweeps into the high bank that I had been told the salmon rested.

My tackle was trout tackle, because it was all I had at the time. My fly was a dry fly, since I had settled in my own mind that that was the best lure for the prevailing condition of low water. Never having caught a salmon, and with practically none being caught at the time, the whole venture had an air of unreality about it.

The deep water at the head of the pool was blacker than ever with the sun slanting down on it from behind me. I cast out again and watched the little ball of fluff that was my Gray Bivisible ride lazily along on the choppy surface where the current was swiftest. Up from the blackness a long dark shape began to materialize. It drifted slowly upward toward the fly. A foot below the surface the salmon was entirely visible. The sun shone on his spotted gill covers, reflecting brightly, as with infinite slowness his nose pointed upward and he sucked the fly down. This was not the famed head and tail rise I had been led to expect. There was no splash of water, no flaring of fins and tail. The fly disappeared and, with every inch of him visible, the salmon sank slowly until he was just a dark shadow again. Reality descended on me with a rush and I raised my rod.

That movement was the signal for the wildest, fastest action I had ever had on a fly rod. The salmon swept down the pool in a magnificent run, featured by three beautiful leaps, and carried out the major part of my hundred yards of backing. Then, suddenly, he was opposite me, leaping and twisting in the fast water while I reeled frantically in an effort to get the great belly out of my line. For the next ten minutes there were leaps and surges and a lot of vicious head shaking. It was the hard, stubborn fight of a fresh run salmon less than five miles from salt water. After his last leap, the eleventh, I worked him in close enough to see him plainly. My wrist was feeling the strain put on it in using a five-ounce rod. I was all set to bring him in to gaff when he started off again wildly on the longest run of the fight.

This was not a steady sweep but a bulldogging series of short rushes, using the current to help take him downstream. *Zing—zing—zing* went the reel until I wondered if he would stop short of the end of my backing. Following downstream as he went, I was able to hold even and finally to gain back line. When he came into the shallow water again he was too weak to leap. He showed the silver of his side and my gaff struck home. In a few seconds she was stretched out on the pebbly bar, a twelve-pound fresh-run female, silvery and bright, bearing the telltale sea lice, dark on the shining scales. She was really a beauty!

Two years later on another stream I watched Victor Coty kill his first salmon taken on light tackle and a dry fly. Victor, my wife, and I were fishing the Little River of Cape Breton at the time.

Little River is as riotous as the Margaree is peaceful. Although only thirty miles from the Margaree in its broad meadows between the hills, this stream pours from one cauldron into another or races through a rocky bed between towering cliffs. Again the water was low, and after the long hike up the river in the heat of the day, we reached the pool below the second falls tired and hot. While Victor and I were putting our tackle together, my wife decided to cool off with a dip in one of the small pockets below the pool. It was she, sitting wet and refreshed on a rock near the tail of the pool, who called, "There's a rise." We watched and again there was a rise. This was the familiar head and tail rise, and it came again and again with about the frequency of a lazy, old brown trout feeding on insects. On the third cast of the Brown Bivisible there came the same arching curve and flash of fins. Vic was fast to his first salmon. The fish rushed up the long pool to the foot of the falls. I hurried over to where the movie camera was set up and then scaled a small cliff to get movie shots from above. I couldn't see Vic, but I watched his line and listened for his shout, "He's coming up," so that I could get set for the jumps. Even though I couldn't see him I knew what a thrill he was getting. As the fish began to tire and dropped back to the lower end of the pool, I gave up my position of vantage and took up a new one where I could see both fisherman and fish.

Vic was having his troubles along with his thrills. In the center of the current at the tail of the pool was a large boulder, partly submerged. Toward this the salmon kept boring steadily. It looked as if the leader might be cut on the sharp edges of this rock until Vic solved the problem by wading out and climbing up on top of it. From there he was able to keep his line free.

That was a thrilling battle to watch. It was a splendid feat of streamcraft, too, since Vic's rod was eight feet long and weighed only three-and-three-quarter ounces. Through the viewfinder of the movie camera I watched that little rod subdue eleven pounds of silver strength. At the end, the salmon was so utterly exhausted that Vic was able to "tail" him with his hand.

When I see those movies they bring back vividly the wild beauty of Little River and the enchantment of a first light-tackle salmon, so different from a fish taken on a heavy, two-handed rod. The close-ups of Vic show the obvious excitement and thrill that was his. How grand it would be if all our precious moments could be preserved in this way. Victor was fortunate that his salmon was caught in the full sunlight of midafternoon and not in the dusk of morning or evening when the camera could not have taken a record of the event.

Another salmon that Victor and I are not likely to forget was caught on the Ecum Secum River in eastern Nova Scotia. Because of low water conditions there were very few salmon up the river but a great many of them in the brackish water to go up on the first rise. The Nova Scotians never fished that spot because of a confirmed belief that salmon could not be caught there. There were plenty of salmon putting on a regular leaping circus in that brackish water to tantalize us, however. But it was not until the village idiot came down and caught a three-pound sea trout that we were courageous enough to fly in the face of tradition and fish there. The first day we did the unheard-of and landed three grilse, and on the following day I landed a salmon. From then on salmon fishing in the brackish water became a popular sport for the local fishermen. Vantage points for fishing were so few that there was often quite a crowd at one spot or another.

The news brought out all the youthful Ike Waltons as well as the seasoned veterans. We used to smile at the tackle with which the kids fished. Their rods ranged from broomsticks and broken-and-mended trout rods to homemade rock-maple rods with wire guides. Their reels were the smallest of trout reels with a bit of line or string on them, twenty-five yards at most. We looked forward to the time when one of them would hook a salmon and predicted a *zing* of the reel followed by the snap of a breaking line.

One afternoon, while Vic and I were leaning against a fence

at one of the hot spots talking with some of the local weather prophets about the possibility of rain, we heard a shout. The shout came from a red-haired youngster who was one of the most avid of the small-reel brigade. "Hi! I've got a salmon," he called. We remembered him particularly because we had been warned that he was always borrowing rods and things. We had also been told that he had several salmon to his credit, however, and we were anxious to see how he did it. The little rod he held in his hands bent almost double as the reel started to sing with the first long rush. Vic and I began to smile broadly. *Zing—zing* went the reel. We waited. The reel continued to sing. When it became obvious that more than fifty yards of line must have come off the reel we looked at each other in amazement.

Someone in the back of the crowd shouted. "Hey, Blair! Watch out you don't break your rod."

To which Blair answered, "I don't care. It isn't mine."

I had my rod in my hand. I looked at Vic and watched a sickly expression spread over his face as it dawned on him that Blair had taken advantage of his preoccupation and borrowed his rod for his fishing. No wonder there was no loud snap at the end of twenty-five yards. Vic's face was a study of mixed emotions as he bellowed, "My God! He's got my baby Leonard." He proceeded to direct the landing of the fifteen-pound salmon from that point on.

That solved the mystery of how Blair landed his salmon. After that we did see several of the kids hook salmon, and the fights ran true to form in each case . . . *Z-i-i-n-g—snap.*

The most diverting salmon I ever hooked was also a resident of the Margaree. I lost him and have never felt that I should have caught him anyway.

Right in the widest part of the valley the current cuts into a high bank and slowly works its way into a field, leaving a gravel bar in its wake on the southern side of the river. In order to stop this erosion of his field, Duncan MacDonald, who owns the land, had built a bulwark of piles to hold the river back. The river ignored this bulwark and continued to cut right on into the bank leaving the bulwark timbers jagging out into the water. This pool came to be called the Snag Pool because of these timbers piercing the current and the pieces of sod which kept dropping into the water from the high bank and settling to the bottom in the slower flow at the tail of the pool.

I had fished the pool from the beach side without success for several hours when one of the local fishermen came down along the high bank. We seldom fished from that side because a man on the bank was almost certain to scare the salmon which would then be almost directly under him. This fisherman, however, was using a heavy weight on the end of his line, so I judged that he had on a large fly or hook with a sinker above it and was trying to foul hook one of the fish that were visible from the high bank. At that point I gave up fishing and, wading across the shallows below the pool, I came up along the bank to watch him. He didn't seem to mind my coming over, although there is a heavy fine for the practice of foul-hooking salmon. I stood beside him and counted ten salmon. I watched him hook two of them and lose them, at which I was secretly glad. Then, being out of hooks, the man prepared to leave. I felt that the fish were too frightened to take a fly, so I started down the pool on my way home.

Glancing out over the water as I walked, I was surprised to see a salmon rise. I had been fishing over those fish for hours without seeing a rise and now suddenly one of them was rising! I stripped off some line and started casting. When I had about forty feet of line in the air I let the fly drop on the water about twenty feet short of the salmon that had risen. I started to strip off more line to cast the rest of the way. No sooner had the Bivisible touched the water than the salmon that had risen left his resting place and swam swiftly over to the fly. He took it coming toward me with a sucking noise similar to that sometimes made by a bass taking a bass bug. From my position on the high bank I was able to see everything clearly. For ten minutes I kept the fish in the lower end of the pool where the dangers due to the lumps of sod were minimized by my height above the water. In the end the fish had his way and went upstream in spite of anything I could do to stop him and in spite of the rocks the local fisherman had rained in ahead of him in an attempt to drive him back.

Upstream he went until I felt my line snagged. Reeling in as I walked up the bank, I saw my line go under a large timber—and about eight feet out in the current beyond it was my fish. Hanging precariously to the top of the bank with my left hand, I stood on none-too-secure footing at the water's edge and pushed my rod down into the water in an attempt to loosen the line where it was caught at the leader knot. The net result of this maneuver was to have my tip catch near the line and stick there so that when I drew the rod back only the butt and mid-section came free. The fish meanwhile had remained motionless, so I sat down on the bank to consider. The local fisherman stood beside me and laughed. "I guess if you want him you'll have to swim for him."

I laughed wryly, too, as I watched the fish hang motionless in the current. He was a big fish and I hated to lose him. Then I thought "why not swim?" After all, I certainly wasn't getting anywhere very fast sitting there on the bank. We were alone at the pool, out of sight of everyone but some men who were haying a few hundred yards away in a field.

In no time I had stripped off my clothes and, taking my short gaff, I dropped to the water's edge and plunged in. I hooked the gaff into the timbers to hold against the current while I worked with my right to free the tip joint which was about six feet below the surface. I came up out of breath and slid the tip up on the bank where the local fisherman took it. "He's taken a lot of line," he reported. I took the line in my hand and pulled. It wouldn't give. Then as I relaxed I felt it being pulled out. Again I tried to pull it back but met the same solid resistance. The line would run out through the snag but jammed when I tried to bring it in.

There seemed only one thing to do if I were to get the fish. I dove down again. With my gaff I hung to the submerged timbers till my left hand closed on the line where it came out on the other side of the snag. I loosed the gaff and came up to the surface. Using my legs and my right hand, which held the gaff, I was able to drift slowly down with the current. My left hand slid down along the line. At last I felt the leader loop. I could feel the fish then, too. I was using a nine-foot leader made up of fifteen strands of gut. Mechanically I counted the knots as they passed through my fingers. One—two—three—four—five. My grip on the leader tightened. I lifted the fish toward the top. I slid my gaff forward. I saw the salmon as he came to the surface. There was a mass of foam and white water from his splashing. I poised the gaff—but the leader in my left hand went slack. The fish was gone, much to my disgust.

I swam back to the bank and sat down. Then, because I was dressed for it, or rather undressed for it, I swam out to a willow snag in the deep part of the pool and salvaged two Jock Scotts, a Black Dose and a nine-foot leader in good condition that some unfortunate anglers had evidently hung up there and lost.

[1937]

CHAPTER FOUR

THE ROD BENDER

*O*utdoor-oriented fiction was a common element in many magazines of the 1930s and 1940s, but is unfortunately missing from almost all such magazines today with their increasing emphasis solely on the how-to's and where-to's of fishing and hunting. Wulff wrote and sold a handful of fiction pieces before World War II, of which this is one example. The identity of the central character will be immediately apparent to veteran Wulff readers, and the salmon-fishing tips herein are important even though their fabric is ostensibly fictional.

YOU ASK ABOUT that feller from New York that was up last year.

I guess I was about the only one up here that liked him to begin with, and that was funny too because he was nice lookin' and well mannered. He wouldn't have had any trouble either except that this town has got one thing on its mind most, and that's salmon.

Why, if a man was to hook a salmon down by the old dam now, in two minutes this whole street would be deserted. Somebody could drive up in a van and steal the whole town, and nobody'd be the wiser until that salmon was lost or landed.

This New York feller was tall and slim—not really thin, but slim lookin'. Long legs, and them wadin' pants that come clean up to his armpits. He was trucked out like a whole fishin' tackle store, too. Had a vest with a dozen or more pockets in it and little boxes full of flies in every one of them, and gadgets and doodads tied onto him everywhere.

He stayed at my place. Drove all night to get here from New York, and without even waitin' to have breakfast he wanted to go fishin'. Black, his name was. Homer Black. I walked down to the stream with him when he got his fishin' things on. I liked him. I guess I'd like any man that'd skip breakfast to go fishin', but it wasn't more'n five minutes before he had the whole town mad at him.

It came on like this: As we walked down past the stores I noticed things looked pretty quiet, so I says, "I guess maybe somebody's got hold of a fish," and sure thing when we got to the bridge there was Chick Oliver—he's one of the local lads—fast to a salmon.

Well, sir, we got out on the bridge where we had a good view of things with the rest of the people. I asked one of the boys how long the salmon had been hooked, and it seems he'd been on about ten minutes. He'd jumped once and they figgered he'd go about ten pounds. Chick was usin' a little nine-foot, split-cane rod he got from a mail-order house, and he wasn't puttin' much strain on.

This New York feller kinda got a little restless as the time went by, and the fish just sulked and didn't budge out of that fast water at the head of the pool. Finally he can't stand it, I guess, and he starts talkin' to me loud enough so the fellers around can hear, about how this is all very dull and a poor demonstration of how to play a salmon, and at this rate the fish will be hooked for the rest of the day unless he gets off.

I says: "Chick's usin' pretty light tackle and dassent put much strain on his rod, and he's got that old mill wheel down there to worry about." I noticed while I was talkin' that his rod was smaller and trimmer than Chick's, but I didn't say anything about that. I was riled up about as much as the rest, I guess.

Finally he says: "This is so dull I'm goin' fishin'."

I tried to tell him to wait a while and I'd show him the holes, but off he goes sayin': "I guess there's salmon in here and I'll find 'em myself."

I told him then, a little sharp, maybe, that, man or boy, I'd never left off watchin' a salmon bein' played till it was weighed in at Ebbing's store or got off.

So this Homer Black walks off downstream. I could watch him now and then while Chick's fish was sulkin'. He throws a pretty line, all right, and he picked the right place to fish, too, first crack out of the box. You know how hard it is to tell where salmon will lie in a stream. That's why most sports hire guides for salmon, but they don't bother with them when they're fishin' for trout.

I was just beginnin' to be amazed at his pickin' the one best spot there below the bridge to start his fishin' when Chick's fish jumped and moved upstream a little. Next time I looked downstream again at the New York feller, his rod was bendin' nearly double. When I saw that, I let out a holler.

Well, maybe you can picture that. Here was the whole town out on the bridge and a salmon bein' played above and below. There was a lot of rushin' back and forth from one side to the other to keep an eye on both fish, but after a couple of minutes everybody stayed on the downstream side.

That pool he was fishin' in was full of snags. Most of us wouldn't fish it except when all the other pools were bein' fished, and so we didn't give him much chance of landin' his salmon.

Right at the start I looked at my watch like we always do and it was just ten after ten. Black follows his fish up and down along the bank. I can't figger yet how he kept him out of those snags, but he did somehow.

After about five minutes he waded out into the water. Our river's not very big; and him, with long legs and waders, he could get around in it. It was amazin' to see him. We never thought of wadin' out there, and of course we only had hip boots up here anyway.

Well, sir. He just sort of chased that salmon all over the pool. He never gave him a moment's rest and that little rod of his was bent all the time. I guess about ten minutes had gone by when he takes a tube about three feet long off a hook on his shoulder where it had been hangin', pulls out a spring inside of it and sets up a noose of some sort with it. Come to find out, it was a tailer—something he made himself.

All the time he's fixin' the noose, which is only a second or two really, of course he's watchin' his fish and keepin' a tight line on him. Then he wades around after his salmon some more, keepin' him on a short line. Pretty soon he slips this thing up over his tail and gives a yank and drags his salmon up on the bank—by the tail. I was so surprised, I didn't look at my watch for a minute—when I did, it was twenty-two after ten.

Somebody gave a shout about Chick's fish then, and we all rushed over to his side of the bridge.

Chick's fish had jumped again, but that was all. He settled right back into the fast water and stayed there. Chick was gettin' a little weary by that time so he sat down on a rock.

I broke my rule then and went down to where Black was with his fish. He grinned at me and says: "That didn't take long, did it?" Then he went on down to the next pool and left me holdin' what turned out to be the second largest fish of the season—eighteen pounds of fresh-run salmon. I took it up to the bridge and showed it to the boys up there; but it just seemed to make everybody mad that this New York feller had showed Chick up.

But that wasn't the worst of it. About that time Chick's fish gets gay and scoots down to the tail of the pool, wraps his line once or twice around the mill wheel and jumps, breakin' the leader, while Chick is still standin' at the head of the pool.

Well, sir, it went on like that for the next six days. He caught fish—and landed them all in nothin' flat—just sort of chased them to death, wadin' around after them, keepin' them movin' like a sheepdog with an ornery old ewe. He landed one ten-pound fish in six minutes, and he was usin' a leader about as fine as the hair on your head. He lost a few, of course. Nobody could land them all in a stream like this with snags and everything.

The town people wouldn't talk to him—just a frosty sort of "How do" when they passed him. He didn't seem to mind much, though. He didn't have time to worry about it, I guess. I never saw a man so eager to fish and so satisfied not to do anything else. He never would have eaten anything or come to bed, I suppose, if it hadn't got too dark to fish at night.

Anyway, the climax of the whole thing came the day he left. It was up at the railroad bridge where you fished today. There was quite a crowd because the biggest fish that's been in here in years was up there.

Y'see, off that railroad bridge you can look down into the water, even if it *is* brown, and see the salmon where they lie at the tail of the pool. It's the only pool in the river where you can do that, too.

We were all anxious to get that fish because the Machias and all the other rivers along the coast have had bigger fish caught in them than we've caught here, so we wanted that salmon for the records. I swear, mister, he'd have gone thirty-five pounds.

Anyway, this Mr. Black set to work on this fish. He got on a high point of bank where he could see the salmon and began to cast. We never fished from there because we never thought of it, I guess, or else we couldn't cast that far. Usually, when we fished we'd get down near the water and cast out with somebody up on the bridge to tell us if we were castin' over the fish or not.

Black started at sunrise and put in the mornin' over that fish.

Every time the big feller would move, Black's fly would follow him and come swimmin' by in front of him time and again.

I was standin' there watchin' that fly of his go over that salmon time after time until I got to wonderin' which of them would go crazy first, Black or the salmon, when suddenly up came the salmon and grabbed the fly.

I never saw a prettier sight than Black playin' that fish. From the bridge I could see every move the salmon made. Black stayed up on the high bank and played him to a standstill in no time, lettin' him run when he had to, but always keepin' him movin'. Pretty soon I saw him stop the fish in one of his rushes, and pull him backwards so he turned on his side.

Then, first thing you know he turned him over on his side again. When that happens a fish is pretty well licked; and I saw then that Black was gettin' his tailer gadget ready. He was just startin' down the bank to finish him when Mr. Salmon turns and swims right toward Black and opens his mouth two or three times in quick succession—and the fly just lifted right out of his mouth.

I went over to where Black was standin' and said "Tough luck" or somethin' like that, although there's nothin' you can say that means anything when a man loses a salmon like that.

Black just stood there lookin' at the fly he'd hooked him on. It wasn't any bigger than my little fingernail, either, and says to me:

"Well, George, a man can't catch them all." He didn't cuss or act mad. He just shrugged his shoulders and took down his rod.

An hour later, when he left for the city, half the townsfolk was out to see him and shake his hand and tell him how sorry everybody was he'd lost that big fish.

Yes, sir, that feller certainly left his mark on this river. The boys are all usin' little flies like he did and long fine leaders. Nobody ever plays a salmon more than half an hour any more. Some of the boys have even sent away and got those rubber wadin' pants.

[1938]

CHAPTER FIVE

THE CONVERSION OF SAMUEL SHINNIX

*B*y the time this chapter was first published in 1944,
Wulff had started working for the Province of Newfoundland,
exploring, filming and promoting its hunting and fishing. Here
we start to meet the delightful people of backcountry Newfoundland such as Sam Shinnix, who figures in this and other chapters.
Dry-fly fishing for Atlantic salmon was still in its infancy in those
years and so were the now-famous Wulff drys, having been developed by Lee during the winter of 1929–30.

I mentioned in this book's introduction how the chronology
of these chapters reflects both changes in attitude and fishing
tactics over the years, and there's a good example here of just
that: a loon being killed as a possible source of fly-tying feathers.

Now that loon populations are threatened in many areas, such an act would be a travesty. Sixty years ago, however, it was taken as a matter of no great consequence.

AWAY UP near the northern tip of the island of Newfoundland lie two salmon rivers, by name, the Torrent River and the River of Ponds. They are a long, long way from the beaten paths of travel, but their inaccessibility is more than equaled by the rumors that whisper them into the mythical spot at the head of all the big island's rivers. For five years they were on my projected itinerary; and each year, for some perfectly logical but equally deplorable reason, my plans had to be changed and that particular trip was postponed. When the chance did come, it came with a rush.

I was in Corner Brook and had just finished one job and was waiting to take another when Frank Silver, manager of the paper mill there and fellow member of the Newfoundland Tuna and Swordfish Club, said, "Lee, things are breaking so that I can get away for a week. Let's go fishing."

"Okay, but where?"

"Well, where do you think the fishing would probably be best right now?"

"I'd say the Serpentine. Or, better still, the Torrent and River of Ponds, if there's any way for us to get there. Those northern rivers have been on my list for a long time, but it's 150 sea miles from here, and Lord only knows how we can get there and back and have much fishing in less than three weeks."

"If we can get down north at all, the best we'll do is four or five days' fishing out of seven," mused Frank, "but I'm game. I need to get away from this mill for a while. My fishing gear is easy to throw together, and I could be ready to go by tomorrow morning."

He picked up the phone on his desk and called the railway that operates the coastal steamers. When he put the phone down, we were smiling. The steamer that travels from Corner Brook to St. John's was due to leave the following morning on her monthly swing around the northern half of Newfoundland. With the problem of getting down there settled, we began to pack and worry about getting back. I sent out a few wires, one of which bore fruit later.

For twelve dollars and a few odd cents each we shared the deluxe cabin on the ship, traveling in complete comfort and with no untoward incident. The following afternoon we ambled down the gangplank at Port Saunders, our port of debarkation for the rivers of our choice. We carried waders, packsacks, rod cases, sleeping bags and duffel bags and had all the distinguishing marks of "sports." We parked the first load and went back aboard for the balance. As we stepped off the gangplank for the second time a burly chunk of a man, built like a fullback and wearing, in addition to his nondescript clothes, an overhanging nose, a ruddy complexion and a wide grin, drifted up beside us.

"I see you got some rods there, gentlemen," this character said. "Are you coming to fish the River of Ponds? I'm Sam Shinnix, and I can guide you."

"Well, not today," said Frank. "But we'll be along there in a couple of days. We're planning to try the Torrent first."

Momentarily Sam showed disappointment, but he was silent for only a second. Then he began his sales talk for his home river.

"The Torrent's a good river, all right, but not like ours," he began. "We live right at the mouth, and we can put you up, guide you and everything. We've got dories and cabins on the good pools, and the river's pretty good right now, even if it is almost August." He carried on in glowing terms and in an accent that was as Irish as the twinkle in his eye, ending up minutes later with: "I see ye've got good tackle. Well, now, wouldn't I like to see you casting your flies out over Clarke's Stiddy. There's salmon in there that will go thirty pounds, and thirty-five—yes, and forty pounds, too, if you can raise 'em and hold 'em. Only a gunshot from my house and as sweet a bit of water as there is on this island, gentlemen."

"Sam," I said, breaking in when he stopped for breath, "how's the river for dry flies?"

He stopped with his mouth partway open, closed it slowly, then opened it up again fast with: "Dry flies, did you say? I've wore out dry flies casting 'em on that river. The fish'll rush on 'em, all right, but they won't take. I s'pose I've hooked fifty of 'em accidental like, but never saved a one. I finally threw all my dry flies away. No, sir, you can't catch 'em on dry flies, but, mister, have you got any small Jock Scotts or Silver Grays?"

Fixing him with my fiercest glare, I said, "We're coming over to your river on Sunday, and I'm going to make you eat those words."

"You come and bring your wet flies. I bet this gentleman's got wet flies," he added, looking toward Frank, "and I know where the salmon are that will take 'em."

We fished the Torrent, and both of us had fun with the big salmon of that river, even though we had one day of intermittent thundershowers and general high-water conditions. And we had another stroke of luck. One of my wires had caught up with Norman Parsons, whose boat I had used for tuna fishing several years before. He called in for us at the Torrent, and we forthwith folded our tent and moved aboard the forty-foot cruiser to live.

We had luck in getting to the River of Ponds, too. That river empties into the Gulf of St. Lawrence on a straight shore, and there is no anchorage except for small boats of limited draft that can get into the river's tidal pool and anchor there. We beat a storm in across the bar by a few hours on the appointed Sunday morning, for when the high waves lash in no boat can cross that shallow bar of sand while the river piles up across its mouth. But we did get there in time and slid in through the channel and dropped our anchor as Sam Shinnix and his gang came down from the group of houses to help us make the guy lines fast to the shores.

Clarke's Steady is just a hop, skip and a jump from the houses. In it the river pushes its brownish flow through a wide arc, deep against the far bank, gradually becoming shallow toward the inside shore of the curve. The pool is long, sweeping along smoothly for more than 200 yards, and it looked fishy all the way. We sat on the boulders near the tail of the pool to slip on our waders and rig up our rods. In the process I tossed one of my big #4 White Wulffs over to Sam, who looked at it curiously.

"You ain't going to put that thing on, be ye?" he asked.

I nodded.

Frank was set up and had already tied on a wet fly under Sam's approving eye. Without a word Sam got up and headed Frank up to a favored spot some distance up the pool, muttering meanwhile: "That guy is going to scare every salmon in the river with that sea-gull fly of his. Might just as well float a whole chicken down over their heads."

Some of Sam's kids and their young companions had installed themselves as a gallery on the far side of the stream, watching all our movements intently. When they saw the big white fly flutter out to midstream and settle down to ride the oily water's surface, they doubled up with laughter. Three casts later, when a fish nosed up and bumped it into the air without taking it or being hooked, they laughed even harder. On the cast that followed, when the same fish sucked it down and then flip-flopped into the air preparatory to his first run, they howled anew with mirth.

When I brought that small salmon in and picked him up with a grip around the tail, I walked over to Sam, who was seated on a grassy patch of bank, and taunted: "So they won't take a dry fly, Sam? This one has taken it down past his tonsils. I think you'd better dig the hook out."

Silently Sam worked the hook out and then, holding the fly before him, looked at it again with wonder. Abruptly he said, "Betcha can't do it again."

But I could, and did. Five minutes later I was fast to a fifteen-pounder that skimmed out over the lip of the pool and took me down through some rapid water and rugged going before I could noose him with the tailer. I brought him back and let Sam disengage the hook. Then we gathered some wild iris leaves and made a pictorial background for his photo.

About that time Frank switched to dry flies, too. And we were both either working over interested salmon or actually playing them for most of the next few hours. The kids on the far bank screamed with delight each time a fish rose or leaped.

That night one of Sam's neighbors came aboard for a visit. Salmon flies were scarce up there, and even bare hooks were entirely unobtainable. So Steve, knowing that we tied flies and perhaps had some hooks along, came over to see what he could wrangle for some feathers. Just to be sure that he wouldn't pass up any feather that might have some value, he had skinned a loon completely, jealously guarding every feather and saving the beak and legs as well. A loon is a mighty big bird, almost as big as a goose. His feathers are a crisp black and white, and to Steve's uninitiated eye they looked as if they should make good salmon flies.

We had just finished our after-dark supper when Steve's dory rubbed gently against our boat. Frank was alone in the stern when this strange, hunched-over little man came aboard. He spoke to Frank in a husky voice, asking if loon feathers would make good flies. Frank couldn't get what he was driving at and simply stared at him in the dim light. So Steve, to clear up the situation, reached inside his shirt and pulled out the almost life-like loon skin and laid it gently on Frank's lap, saying again, "Sir, are these feathers any good for making flies?"

Frank's description of this great loon skin materializing from inside the little man's shirt, like something alive, was worth listening to! Unfortunately, loon feathers are square-ended and not particularly suitable for flies, but Steve left us with a few flies and hooks so that he could resume his salmon fishing. And just to keep things even, he brought us gifts of fresh eggs daily.

The next two days fairly flew by on wings—dry-fly wings. Sam showed us his river and its salmon lies, the cabins he had built and all points of special interest. He had a sparkle and good humor that never seemed to leave him. Every fish we brought in seemed to thrill him anew, and each one was always a "perfect fish." We kidded him unmercifully about having heaved all his dry flies away, but agreed to leave a stock of them with him at the very last moment before our departure.

We spent much of our time at Clarke's Steady because of its convenience and the beauty of its fishing water. And we found that even on that almost unfished pool the salmon had their moods; after the first foolish fish either were taken or had their lesson in how to behave at the end of a leader, the going grew tougher. Soon we really had to work for our fish, and they were more skittish. This is especially true of dry-fly fishing, where a fair percentage of rises are missed and each miss leaves behind it a salmon warier than he was before.

It's strange that out of a poolful of fish only certain ones have the urge to rise at all, and that the same few fish seem to lift toward the fly time after time. So it was that we had five or six good salmon "marked down" in their various lies. The water of the River of Ponds is tinged with the brown of peat bogs, and our eyes couldn't pierce its depths to see the fish, but we learned that a fly fished over a certain spot brought up a fish from below. Nine times out of ten he rose short or just slid up under the fly for a look-see. Sometimes it would mean seeing a flash of silver deep down, and sometimes a salmon would lift easily till he all but broke the surface and came into full view.

Another thing about dry-fly rises is that a fair percentage of fish prefer to take a fly after it has passed over them by swinging around and moving downstream on it. A salmon really has to mean business to be hooked on this type of rise, as any striking by the angler tends to pull the fly out of the fish's mouth, and no strike at all seldom hooks a fish, either. So we entered a stage of fishing that is at once exasperating and satisfying. We worked over individual fish, and the way they would look over a fly or swirl at it without taking it explained why Sam, under similar conditions, might have come to believe that the fluffy floaters wouldn't work.

Things finally slowed down to a point where Sam's faith in the wet fly revived again. Of course, he hadn't been fishing while guiding us, and the poorer the fishing grew the slyer the twinkle in his eye became. When action was slowest, just at the tail-end of the afternoon, he offered to follow me on a given stretch of water and in an equal amount of time take more or bigger salmon. We chose a twenty-minute period, and I worked like the devil to dig up three short or missed rises and nothing more.

Sam, taking over, borrowed the beautifully balanced twelve-foot rod that Frank had set up but used little since his lighter dry-fly outfit had been in almost continuous action. I've always enjoyed watching old rivermen like Sam fish. They all fish well, and usually productively. Each has his own pet twist or swing, and no two ever seem to be alike unless you run into a river where everyone is standardized into a given pattern. Perhaps I should say that the men of no two rivers fish identically. One thing, however, will be certain: They'll know their water.

Those of us who fish widely on varying types of water learn a lot that the one-river man never learns, but there will be few pools that we'll ever know as Sam knows Clarke's Steady. He fished this spot and then that one, instead of covering the water more or less generally as we did. His #8 Silver Gray slid along just where he wanted it to. I fished dry because I like to watch the big fellows come to the surface and because conditions were much better for dry flies than for wet ones, but that didn't mean the latter wouldn't work, especially when fished as Sam was fishing his. Almost unbelievably, minute after minute went by until Sam's quota was spent without moving a fish.

His time over, Sam sat down beside me and lamented that something was wrong with the river for the fishing to be so poor, and "must be there's a storm coming up." Frank, who had been talking with me, got up and started tossing one of my gray flies on a #10 hook out over the lie of a salmon we had raised more than a dozen times and hadn't once touched with the steel. Three casts, and he sloshed up from the brown depths and nailed the little floater. Frank, busy as he was, had time to remark that it wasn't every fisherman who was really qualified to say when the fishing was or wasn't good on a particular stretch of water before he needed all his breath to follow his fish downstream. I changed from white bucktail wings to brown, just for luck, and started fishing again.

We had the river to ourselves and were the first outsiders to fish it in several years, but the shadow of the future loomed large on the third day when an R.A.F. amphibian dropped down into a half-mile-wide pond that lies in the river's flow. Its crew proceeded to catch a few salmon and then piled back into their plane and whisked up into the sky again. No river with ponds in its length, or nearby, and lying within reach of small planes from inhabited centers, will ever again be as isolated as the River of Ponds has been. Corner Brook lay only an hour's flight away.

The wind whistled in from the west that night, and soon the high waves were rolling and roaring in across the bar. Thus we were storm-bound on the day we were due to leave, and there was nothing for us to do but stay another day and fish. Frank fished leisurely at Clarke's Steady and the lower pools. Sam had talked so much about the upper pools that I inveigled him into the long trek upstream.

On this little jaunt we walked two miles and then rowed half a mile in a dory. Next, the dory had to be dragged up through half a mile of rough water bringing us to River of Ponds Pond. We rowed six miles across the big pond. While I bent my back to the oars on the middle thwart Sam kept his straight and pushed his oars from the stern seat "so he could kind of keep us headed right."

We took another trail for three more miles to the smoother section of the upper river and then waded and fished another mile and a half till we reached the forks where the Rising Tilt joins the waters from the lakes that lie in the shadow of Big Bluie Mountain. Here we turned back and repeated the process in reverse. It was dark before we reached the houses at the river's mouth, but it had been a full day—full of travel and full of fishing, for in the limited fishing time I had captured and released fifteen salmon and twice that many trout. As we broke out into the clearing Sam, who had been checking the time quite frequently, asked again.

"It's two minutes to eleven," I replied.

"We're just in time to hear Gabriel [Heatter]," he whispered in a voice greatly hoarsened by a full day of fishing tales, and he guided me through the door into his house and toward the radio.

Frank wrote me that Sam came down to Corner Brook in the fall and got a new string for his fiddle. He was also looking in at all the shops for dry flies, since he had lost all those we gave him. Frank writes, too, that Sam asked him to tell me that he's going to put a motorboat up on the big lake so it won't be such a long row to the upper river in case we ever come again. He said to come the first chance we got and be sure to bring our dry flies. I think maybe we will.

[1944]

CHAPTER SIX

CHARLIE'S POOL

*T*he natives of Newfoundland, where this piece from *1946 takes place, have to this day speech patterns so thick with dialect and accent that understanding is at times difficult for those people who "come from away," as the Newfoundlanders call those from the outside. As Wulff points out in a later chapter, one characteristic is the addition of an "h" to words beginning with a vowel, and the dropping of the "h" in words that begin with that letter. Thus the word "owl" becomes "howel" in this chapter, where Wulff's sharp ear for dialect makes the story all the funnier.*

WE WATCHED CHARLIE move on ahead, wading the canoe up-stream through the rough water, and saw the swirling waves rise to his ample middle. Pfc. Carl Lowe of Portland, Oregon, a member of the Search and Rescue Unit of a nearby U.S. Army airfield, stood beside me. For a few minutes we watched him make his way into that rugged, boulder-strewn stretch of water. Then we turned into the woods to take a path that would lead us back to the river a mile and a half upstream at the first salmon pool, a swirling scoop of twisting water that had been gouged out of solid stone. On a previous trip I had waded up through that rough river bed to the first pool, and there was no need of our scrambling over the submerged rocks this time, when a good trail would take us there quickly and dry-shod.

We were headed up a river that will be nameless, a long river that rises far back in the high lake country over which the big silvery C-54s flew on their last long hop across the North Atlantic after refueling at the field. For me it meant a scouting trip to determine what that rarely fished river and the area through which it flows had to offer in the way of a postwar tourist en-terprise that would provide work and a fair return for their efforts to some Newfoundland members of the allied forces. For Carl it meant an opportunity to familiarize himself with some wild country through which he might have to travel, either by canoe and on foot in the summer or with his team of nine Siberian huskies in the winter, in the event one of those big planes ever faltered in this section of their flight.

Charlie knows this river better, in all probability, than any other living man. He made his first trip up the river to the lakes at the age of fourteen, and now at sixty-seven he was still traveling the woods, portly of figure, gray of locks, and no longer able to pick up 400 pounds and walk all day under its load. "The best has long since gone out of me," Charlie is wont to say. But while we walked the trail in comfort he was sure-footedly jockeying the canoe and our stuff up a stretch of river too tough for any canoeman to pole up through in the normal manner.

I had my light fly rod with me, and I fished the head of the pool for the fifteen minutes it took Charlie to catch up with us. The early September sun was clouded over, and the chill that comes with the northern fall cut through our clothing when the wind gusted down on us from upstream. It was time for the salmon to be up near the headwaters, anyway, except for those few stragglers that might have missed their cue and come in very, very late. No such fish rose to my fly from out of the deep, dark water; but when Charlie stopped beside us in the canoe, he said, in his soft French accents, "Ha! I scare out one, maybe two big salmon by the tail of the pool when I come across. Bright like I guess they just come in."

From there on up the river was new to me, and we waded the shoreline while Charlie continued to wade and nurse the loaded canoe up through another two and a half miles of water too rough for poling. Beyond that distance we had hopes of all getting into the canoe and traveling more normally. It had been this barrier of rough water near the river's mouth that had kept it free of anglers for so many seasons.

The alders hung out over the edge of the stream and, although the river was low, it was impossible to wade its edges without getting wet between the knees and the hips. To break through the network of alders and blown-down spruce and fir trees was a much slower and more laborious job. It was better to be wet than to fight through that tangle of branches.

Our start up the river had been in early afternoon. At six o'clock we made camp at the head of the rough water, a sketchy camp on a beach of sand and small gravel—the first piece of dry sand we'd seen on the riverbed up to that point. We had come with light equipment, for there were three of us in one canoe. Our equipment was G.I. I had left my heavier sleeping bag behind in favor of half of one of the Army's lightweight arctic type. Carl slept in the other half, and Charlie, too, had another single section. Beneath us and above us went light waterproof tarps, gaudily orange on one side and blue on the other, a bit of search-and-rescue salvage from a wrecked plane's ditching equipment.

Before we hit the sack after our evening meal, Carl and I

walked downstream a hundred yards and cast our flies into a small rocky pool that didn't seem to give much promise. In the end, however, it produced for me a five-pound grilse, or Atlantic salmon of only one year's sea feeding, and a sea-run squaretail trout that weighed about a pound and a half. I saved the trout and put the small salmon back into the water with our blessings. Carl's fly drew no fish for him, which may have been because there were no others left in the pool or because, with the season well advanced, the fish were dour and had little interest in anyone's flies. I knew, though, that before the trip was out Carl would be grinning.

That night, as we slept on the beach over small hollows made to fit our hips and shoulders, a hard driving shower blew big wet drops in under our seven-by-seven waterproof cover. In our birthday suits Carl and I got up and gathered the supplies in a pile between us and stretched the small cover over all three of us and the supplies, managing to keep reasonably dry. The short rain passed on down the river with the wind, and then the stars came out again. Morning grayed in with more heavy clouds, and the drone of the C-54s, passing unseen above us, was loud in our ears when they went over.

Now that the river had leveled off in the smoother flow, we hoped to ride the canoe; but the river, almost ninety yards wide on the average, was filled with shallow stretches lacking depth for the loaded canoe, and our rides between them would have been mighty short. Consequently, we waded on as before, hugging the alder banks when we could, wading up the shallow center of the river when the water cut in deep against the banks. In that way we covered another two miles of stream.

We passed the Hayrock and came around a bend to sight a long, slow-moving pool that ran, deep and steady, in an arc almost 200 yards long. I caught my breath a second when I first saw it clearly. It's such a pool as anglers dream of, perhaps as fine as the Grand Codroy's Forks Pool, which is generally considered Newfoundland's best. Charlie drew up the canoe beside me and said softly, "Campbell's Pool."

The whipping wind of the previous day had caused me to don long underwear that I'd brought with me, just in case. I had appreciated it during the wading up the river; now, with better going ahead, I decided to shed my trousers, which were completely wet, and hang them by Charlie's fire on the beach to dry. While the trousers were drying I waded out, in my underwear, to try to catch a salmon.

I had flown over the river to the upper waters, the myriad lakes in which it rises, where almost all of its salmon run should be by this time. Twice before I had tried to get up the stream by canoe, but each time conditions had been bad. Once it was a raging torrent, much too high to travel, and the second time it had been almost bone-dry and the shallows were too tough to take a canoe through.

Even though I'd seen that wealth of water at the river's head, I knew that such a beautiful pool with its gravelly shores and shallow water at the tail end of the arc would hold some fish that should stay on and spawn there, even though 99.99 percent of the run had gone on upstream. And, having been in fresh water for at least a month, they would have lost that fidgety edge which seems to make salmon rise to the fly. They'd be more cautious, less curious and darned hard to catch.

We sent our flies out over the swift, shallow run at the head of the pool. There, in the shallower flow, our flies would not be so far above the streambed and consequently would pass closer to the heads of the salmon lying just above the pool's rocky floor. Being closer to the fish, they'd be more tantalizing. Carl fished a small wet fly of silver body and black squirreltail that he had made up on a #10 hook. I let a dry fly on the same size hook float lazily along on the water's choppy surface. Late season for salmon usually demands small flies. Six weeks earlier we'd have been using fours or sixes instead.

Three fish flashed up at my floating fly and looked it over at close range before heading back to their lies without opening their mouths. One swirled behind Carl's fly, but failed to close his jaws on the combination of fur and tinsel and steel. Then, just when Charlie was singing out, "Come on, she's ready!" one poked his nose up over the Gray Wulff and as he dove the hook went home.

The fish was a grilse, and he threw his five-pound weight around with the usual abandon. I balanced it with the pressure of the delicate fly rod and spurred him on to waste his strength as quickly as I could. After they've been in the river a bit the salmon are not so wild on their runs. The memory of the limitless space of the ocean isn't so strong with them, and they fight a different sort of battle. They may leap as much as ever, but they're used to the stream and they look where they're going. They don't run themselves into awkward spots that require another immediate waste of their strength in a long run back to the safety of the deep water. They're far more stubborn, and it may take longer to bring in a September fish than his twin caught in June or July.

This one was no exception. He fought a hard fight, and Carl and Charlie were well into the corn and beans before I brought him in beside me in the knee-deep flow. Reaching down with my open hand, I let my thumb and second finger go over the back of his neck and find the sockets just behind his forward fins. Gripping him tightly then, I lifted him clear of the water and carried him to shore. There I took off my wet unmentionables, put on some normal underwear and my dry pants and dug into the grub with Carl and Charlie.

We pushed on upstream when lunch was over, and this time we all rode. The canoe was Charlie's. We might have had a canoe from the airfield, but Charlie had been set on taking his own instead. "It is," said Charlie, "the best damn canoe I ever put my boots into. And me, I've put my boots into plenty, I tell you."

We were glad enough to get our boots into one, and from then on we traveled upstream through quiet water, sometimes deep and sometimes shallow. The river continued to be hemmed in closely by the mountains through which it flowed, an area that has never been logged over and has all the natural beauty that goes with untouched forests. The sky above stayed dull, and now and then a wisp of cloud would hang not far above us, seeming to be resting on the side of one of the green mountains.

We put up a flock or two of teal, some black ducks and a double brood of mergansers that numbered fifteen young and two old ones. Then we put up a great horned owl. The big bird flew about a quarter of a mile ahead and lit in a tree. As we approached his new position he flew a bit farther and settled again. Time after time we put him to flight, and each time he flew up the river for only a short distance. Carl and I began making guesses as to just what moment he'd take to the air again on our approach. Finally Charlie spoke up.

"The funniest thing I ever saw about a howel was up on Birchey Lake," he began. "It was at night, and we were camped beside the water. We had a regular tent with only a short piece of stovepipe that came just through the top. The fire was hot, and the flames and sparks came up above the pipe for maybe a foot and a quarter. And do you know what that crazy howel did? He had to come and pitch right on top of that."

"Did he burn up, Charlie?" I asked quickly. "Did it kill him?"

"No, sir, but he let out a big squawk and flew off all squinged."

That night we camped above the dark waters of the Seal Pool. It rained again about midnight, and there was another quick scramble to make sure everything was under cover and dry. Just before dawn, while the night was still soft and black, I found myself sitting bolt upright, with the sound of a big salmon's leap ringing in my ears. The fish jumped again, not more than thirty feet from me, and the sound was like a thunderclap in the ghostly silence.

I lay awake listening to Carl's even breathing and Charlie's healthy snores for a few minutes, and I thought of the big salmon this river must hold somewhere up in these pools or on beyond. The coming day, I knew, would find Carl fastened to a good many trout and salmon and would bring him the accomplishment of one of his ambitions—the capture of an Atlantic salmon.

I was right. The real thrill came when we rounded the bend two miles farther upstream and Charlie said: "Here is my pool.

Charlie Bennett's Pool! The best damn pool on the whole ree-vurr!"

And so we found it. We dropped our wet flies out into the shimmering current and let the moving water swing them back toward shore. Following behind, I watched Carl's rod bend hard after a few casts, and a salmon heading downstream drew a long scream from his reel. On the edge of the dark alders the fish made his first leap, sending a white pattern of spray fanning out above him. Carl went downstream with him and let the fish work back and forth in the current until he could be guided toward a downstream eddy where the water was black and still.

The fish leaped and drew line off the reel in repeated sizzling rushes until his strength was spent. Then, when he was almost all in, he doggedly worked upstream, almost to the point from which Carl had hooked him. Carl beached the nine-pound salmon gently on the gravelly shore. The smile that went with the playing of that fish didn't wear off all day, and I think it must flash on every once in a while when he thinks of Charlie's Pool.

We started through the pool again, and a fish of about fifteen pounds came up and engulfed Carl's fly. The next cast I saw a heavy swirl behind my own fly and felt the line tighten. A salmon that I judged at twenty-five pounds rocketed out of the water and headed down for the deeper part of the pool. We were both busy enough, each with his own problems, for a while. Then Carl's line went slack and his grin faded. I turned a minute later to see him looking ruefully at the end of a very empty leader. Shaking my head in sympathy, I waded on down below him. Then, as Carl came down beside me with his camera set, I said, "I think he's coming out of the water again any second now."

He did, but not where Carl had the camera pointed. And that, I think, was the last jump for the day, because he and the #10 Jock Scott parted company in the air and we both stood there shaking our heads.

We hooked other salmon, caught them, released them and went on fishing. We were busy rising, hooking or playing fish all day long, but there wasn't another moment to compare with the one when we'd each had on a big salmon, and none of those we caught later could equal them for size. About noon we headed downstream toward our Seal Pool camp, fishing as we went.

At the Beaver House Pool, Charlie showed Carl a spot where almost every cast meant a strike from a big sea-run squaretail, and Carl caught them until he was tired of it. Late that afternoon we were back at Seal Pool. We didn't go above Charlie's Pool. Beyond it lay a long stretch of rough water with very few pools of any size in it. We hadn't time to make the long hike past that stretch to the upper waters where, at that season, the bulk of the salmon should be. But now that the war is over, it should provide real sport for anglers who will come from all over the world to fish this up-to-now unknown river.

[1946]

CHAPTER SEVEN

FLIGHT TO THE RIVER OF PONDS

*T*he River of Ponds in Newfoundland is only a few
miles from Portland Creek, where Wulff started a salmon camp
in 1946, the same year in which this essay first appeared. At the
time of this chapter, he was also continuing his Newfoundland–
Labrador explorations that took place in part with the military
stationed there during World War II and in part as a means of
developing recreational opportunities for the military in the Far
North. This led in those years to fishing expeditions with the
likes of Generals Hap Arnold, who started the Army Air Corps,
and George Marshall, who eventually won a Nobel Prize for his
work on the reconstruction of Europe after the war.

OFF TO THE EASTWARD lay some of the toughest country a man would want to look at, let alone get lost in. A plateau that leveled off at better than 2,000 feet had been so cut up by the receding ice cap that it looked incredibly desolate and forbidding. The timber stopped at about 1,200 feet, and above that there was some scrubby growth, but mostly gray rock accentuated by the patches of snow that the mid-July sun had not yet melted.

Below us the land was level and well wooded, punctuated by big lakes that seemed to drain the valley which had been hollowed out of the rock barrier to our right. We swept along over water and forest at about 130 miles an hour with the roar of the motor in our ears and an eagerness within us to see the big pond for which we were headed.

Corner Brook lay behind us. Westward to our left the Gulf of St. Lawrence shimmered and moved restlessly under a light westerly wind and received the drainage of the high slopes of Newfoundland's long northern peninsula. I checked the big lakes off as we passed each one: Western Brook Pond, St. Paul's Inlet, Parson's Pond, Portland Creek and, finally, River of Ponds. We lost altitude as we nosed over the six-mile spread of River of Pond's Big Pond and roared down the valley over the lower river as it wound its way through the two-and-a-half-mile run from the big pond down to the salt water. At the Tidal Pool we banked around sharply, watching the figures on the shore and taking in the clean white lines of Frank's cabin cruiser, the *Gertrude*, moored there in the flow.

Back over the big pond again Howard Maxwell, Lieutenant Colonel U.S.A.A.F., brought the single-motored Grumman amphibian down to the lake's level and slid her along the surface toward the shore. Wheels down, she felt the sandy bottom and drove along until she was close enough for us to wade ashore. We had hardly set the anchors when we saw figures moving up the far side of the stream, where it emptied from the lake.

They were two lads whom Frank had sent up from the river's mouth, and they dug a hidden dory from the alders and rowed across to greet us. We crossed back with them in the dory while the lingering sunlight faded. Soon we were headed down the trail toward Frank's cruiser, stopping briefly half a mile below at the Officer's Pool.

The river splits into two main currents where it enters a small round pond at this point, and in each of the flows, where the swift water loses some of its force and the bottom drops away a bit, the salmon lie. We should have hurried on down the trail, but there was something too tempting about that pool in the twilight. We rigged up and fished briefly, although the gathering darkness urged us to go on down the remaining two miles while there was still light enough to see.

A big salmon rose once to Howard's fly and was pricked lightly by the hook. I hooked a five-pound grilse, a small salmon of only one year's sea feeding, and lost him at that first wild leap. Then we continued downstream along the trail.

By the time we reached the river's mouth we were stumbling along in darkness, and the beam that Frank's flashlight sent shoreward from the dim white bulk of the cabin cruiser was more than welcome. Soon we were enjoying warm food and hot tea and Frank and Hal were telling us the high spots of their week of fishing.

The rivers had been high. Atlantic salmon-fishing is often more of an illusion than a sport. The time for their trip had been picked in order to strike the river at its seasonal peak. But, oh, the plans of mice and men!

Mother Nature had stepped in with a week of rain and the rivers had raged down in uncontrollable floods. The result had been perfect conditions for the salmon to climb the long rivers to their ultimate goals at the headwaters, but miserable conditions for the anglers who sought to deceive them with feathers and steel. So it had been slim fishing for them. Except for a small salmon one morning, their first four days had been blanks. When they had cruised farther north, they put in a blank morning on the Torrent. An eighteen-pounder, weighed by the guide's honest blue eyes, had escaped Hal's hook and the guide's gaff.

But on the day of our arrival, back on the River of Ponds, with the waters somewhat abated, they had both caught a pair of salmon and agreed that the prospects looked good for the morrow. The river had steadied off in its flow, though it remained high. The weather had settled and the glass was steady. There were still plenty of salmon in the pools to provide good fishing.

The boat lay just nosing into the river with lines guying it to the bank on either side. While the early morning aroma of coffee and bacon and eggs was mixing with the atmosphere outside the galley, I perched myself on the stern of the *Gertrude* and began casting a long streamer fly into the receding flow. The brownish water, typical of the peat-stained rivers of the North, was sliding easily by to mix with the gin-clear salt water of the Gulf, not far astern.

I had little hope of attracting a salmon, but if fortune was with me I could hope for a rise or two from sea-run squaretail trout, since they usually hang up where the fresh water hits the salt. It was for that reason I had tied on the long silver-bodied yellow-and-white streamer. The big squaretails like a mouthful to rise to. Salmon, on the other hand, rise to very small flies, a six or an eight being the most common size. And salmon rarely rise to flies unless they have settled into their resting places in the pools. Fishing for them in open water is not considered very smart.

Just to prove that all rules are made to be broken, I caught no trout and raised only one lone stray that swirled behind my fly on a long cast. But when the smell of food was too fragrant to ignore and I was making what I thought to be my final cast, a big silvery form lashed up from the brown depths and made a vicious pass at that long streamer. I cast repeatedly to that spot then, presenting flies more suited to the dignity of a salmon, but that single effort must have used up all his curiosity, and I went in to breakfast empty handed. If I'd done things the wrong way— fished for salmon where they shouldn't have been—I might have been successful.

Breakfast over, we headed up to the pools and settled down to fishing. Action was spotty, but we all ran into some. Howard bent into his casting all the strength of his 220 pounds, concentrated high up on his very ample frame. He drove his fly out to the dark middle run of Clarke's Steady and let it swing back with the current.

Howard's guide, a sharp-eyed pirate named Sam, stood beside him. Knowing that Howard was fishing this river for the first time, he began advising him in minutest detail on how to cast and how to make the fly swing in, when to lift it from the water and where to drop it next. Each time he found something to shake his head about. He muttered now and then under his breath.

Meanwhile, Frank had hooked into a fish down below us, and a cast or two later I fastened into a small salmon near the head of the long pool. We both went through the exciting business of playing our fish successfully, and when both fish had leapt themselves out and raced their way to exhaustion Sam was still standing dejectedly by the colonel.

Frank beached his fish at the lower end of the pool, and I reached down and picked mine up by the tail with a grip that closed down on the narrow base where that sturdy fin commences. When it's done right, that tail grip seems to paralyze a fish and hold him motionless until you drop him on the beach. It worked that way this time. It's a good grip, but it takes a fair amount of practice to use it.

Now, when you're commanding officer at an important Army Airfield, you handle a lot of men and, knowing the high regard his men have for him, I believe the colonel will stack up against the next man in that capacity. I don't know what he said to Sam, but whatever it was, the latter must have been convinced that he'd do better somewhere else. I saw him walking toward the shore, his bearing expressive of "The stubborn fool will never catch a fish."

Leaning into the bamboo, Howard sent the line whistling out, and *wham!* He was doing business with a salmon that had his own ideas of how to break free.

Sam never reached the shore. He turned and waded bulkily out to his old stand beside the colonel and "helped" him land that salmon. He worked harder than the colonel did; he sweated out each run the fish made and tensed at each leap. Grinning and clamping down extra hard on the cigar at the corner of his mouth every now and then, the colonel countered the salmon's every move and soon had him hanging on the ropes in the shallow water.

Sam shambled out toward the tired fish, one arm extended, and I could see his open hand poised to duplicate my hand-tailing of a few minutes before. I had lain awake nights worrying out just how to work that grip and make it stick before I dared to try it. When it's done right, it looks so simple that there seems to be nothing to it. Sam's hand plunged down swiftly, and just as swiftly the salmon took line screaming off the reel.

Again the colonel brought the fish in, and again Sam maneuvered himself into position and sent that horny claw of his down in a quick sweep. Spray splashed up into his face, and he tottered back as the salmon sped out once more toward the deeper water.

A third time the tackle brought the salmon close in, and a third time either Sam's quick motion startled the fish or his fingers touched him before they could close completely in a secure grip. Again the salmon started off in a flurry of white water. But his exertions had been great and he was tired. And Sam, his faith in my fancy grip now shattered, resorted to an old, old system. His boot-clad foot caught the fish amidships and lifted him toward the shore where, with a quick follow-up, Sam sent him high and dry.

For another fifteen minutes we were all busy, either playing fish or working on those tough ones that rise short and leave a big boil behind your fly. When one of them rises short, I figure it's an even break that he's misjudged the fly and missed it because of his long period of sea feeding where he didn't have to contend with currents and eddies instead of just deciding at the last minute that he wasn't interested. So I try to duplicate the cast exactly.

I cast the same length of line and at the same angle, and let the wet fly make its smooth and easy swing through an identical arc. When you're casting a long line, an exact duplication of a cast may take some time, but I think that when it happens chances are better than even that your salmon will rise again, this time with a compensation that will take care of his earlier error. I worked two grilse to the steel after false rises in that way. Then everything stopped.

More than an hour went by with none of us having a rise. We fished just as hard and just as skillfully, but the river seemed suddenly empty of salmon. Sam, sensing the lull shortly after it began, retreated to a comfortable spot on the bank and relaxed in dozing silence. Hal and his guide, moving upstream from a lower pool, passed along the trail on the pool's far side and reported one grilse taken at the start and nothing afterward.

The colonel broke the ice again late in the morning, when we were all casting as much for exercise as in hope of hooking a salmon. The fish took the fly going away on a steady surge, and in that instant of astonishment Howard's teeth clamped clear through his stubby cigar. Sam stirred himself and stood at the pool's edge while the salmon made his bid for freedom. When he was wearied to exhaustion by the pace of his runs and the effort of his tumbling leaps, the delicate power of the split bamboo and the grip of the #8 fly at the end of the long tapered leader brought him close to the pebbly beach. Sam warily waited till the fish's head hit the shore and then charged in from astern and scooped him safely out onto the rocks.

Not long afterward it fell to Frank to bring in the biggest fish of the day. A year earlier, in those very waters, Frank had been converted to the dry fly. Now, although conditions were far more favorable to the sinking type, he plugged ahead with his favored floaters. He had moved a fish twice in the deep, dark water near the spot where the pool spills over, but each time the fish had failed to take the bucktail-winged fly into his mouth.

Time passed, and Frank kept on casting. He knew that if he moved to another part of the pool he'd probably hook a fish much sooner, but he had made up his mind to have that particular fish, and in the end he brought him up to the steel.

The third rise was solid, and for the next twenty minutes Frank was busy while an eighteen-pounder emptied a full bag of tricks. Howard and I stopped fishing to watch and listen to Sam's advice, which Frank apparently didn't need too much, because he used so little of it. The salmon was bright and full of life—worth all the effort that Frank put into bringing him up for that final rise. He beached him gently on the pebbly shore a little below the spot where he'd risen to the fly and then, having killed him, washed him off carefully and put him up in the shady grass and covered him with ferns. It was Frank's last day and our only one on the river, and that salmon made a good prize to take home.

Of all the tackle tricks I've pulled in what anyone but an angler might call a largely misspent life, none was quite so unexpected, so next-to-impossible and yet so successful as the one that came off at Officer's Pool that evening. We had said good-bye to Frank and Hal, who by then were already headed down the coast in the cabin cruiser, and were on our way back to the plane for the return flight to the south. Each taking one of the two sweeps of current that pour into the steady water, we had fished them through several times without success. It was past time to go. Howard was wading to shore and I was making that last cast when a five-pound fish latched onto the #8 Jock Scott I had bent to the end of my leader.

I was using the rod I've used for many seasons for practically all my salmon fishing—a two-piece, seven-foot, two-and-a-half-ounce fly rod. The fish worked through a typical battle and was beginning to tire when at last I was able to bring him in close to me. Howard was standing on the bank with a fidgety look that said, "Come on, let's get out of here. It's getting late!"

Perhaps I was forcing the issue a little too much; perhaps I was careless in my hurry. At any rate, I was standing in the quiet water that lay just out of the current, at a depth between my knees and my hips, and the fish was right in front of me. I started to reach out to pick him up and at the same time I lifted him gently with the rod. But he had other ideas.

He flashed between my legs like a silver streak. Before I knew it and without any conscious thought, I let the tip of my light rod follow along behind him and, arching hard, the rest of the rod followed along. Instinctively, my free hand swung around and picked the rod up from the rear as I let the hand that held it go slack. In less than a second I was playing him perfectly again, having passed the rod safely between my legs. Howard gulped and swore, and Sam's eyes bugged out as he stared at me, disbelieving. Nonchalantly, I drew him in again, this time to pick him up with a sure grip behind the forward fins and release him, uninjured, to spawn more salmon for us for another year.

We went on up to the big pond then, and I crossed first in the small dory. While I waited for Sam to bring Howard over on the second trip, I let a Gray Wulff float lazily along with the smooth current that drains the lake into the river at a spot called Broadway by the local fishermen. Two casts, and a dark nose poked up over the fly and pushed it under. A few seconds later a bright big salmon, equally as large as the one Frank had taken, hurtled out into the air and showed me his full silver length. He threw the fly with the same gallant motion and went back to the water a free fish.

In another few minutes we were airborne, heading south for Corner Brook. The low-hanging sun was painting the distant hills on our left with a warm radiance above the Gulf of St. Lawrence to the west. Before it set I was back in Corner Brook, whereas the *Gertrude* didn't reach there for another twenty-four hours.

[1946]

CHAPTER EIGHT

ON DELIVERING AN
IDENTICAL FLY

*T*his *1957 article was written at about the same time as Wulff's second salmon-fishing book,* The Atlantic Salmon, *which appeared in 1958. His first such book, by the way, was* Leaping Silver, *which appeared in 1940. By the late 1950s there was a general shift in outdoor media to an increased emphasis on instruction, which sometimes took place at the expense of angling's basic romance and appeal. This and most subsequent chapters in this book's chronology are representative of that change, but to Wulff's credit he never lost his feeling in print for the sport he loved so much. Even though much of his subsequent writing was been either instructional or an argument for conservation's sake, he always made sure that the rich flavor of angling persisted in his material.*

THERE ARE TIMES when an angler simply fishes an area of water, knowing salmon should be lying within it. In the early season this is a necessary way to fish since the exact lies of the salmon in heavy, floodtime water can rarely be predetermined. Fortunately, under high-water conditions, especially in the case of fresh-run fish, the salmon are fairly willing to rise. As the water level drops and the fish settle into the habitual resting places they have used for generations, this fishing of all the water of a pool becomes less and less productive.

Then the salmon will be gathered in tightly knit groups or pairs or individuals. To fish well for a single salmon or a small group, the fly must be sent to a very special, small area within the pool to catch a fish, and the uniform coverage of the water becomes a very inefficient way to hook a salmon.

Anglers or guides who have had many opportunities to watch a salmon from a vantage point like a bridge or high bank while someone was fishing for it have noticed frequently that a very accurate presentation of the fly to a certain spot is necessary to interest the fish. With a wet fly it is often not only a movement through a particular spot in the salmon's vision at a given distance but in a certain manner.

A resting fish may be seen to rise slightly from the bottom when such a fly passes near. A dozen casts later he may lift again. Usually this will be when the fly comes to him in the same certain way. Often half a dozen false rises will be seen, each to the fly at a certain spot, swimming a particular course. Eventually, if the casting continues the fish is either hooked or pricked by the fly.

This points up the need for accuracy whenever an angler is casting to a fish he has risen. When, as an angler works his way along, a salmon rises and is short, it is time to take stock of the situation at that instant for future reference. The exact length of line out of the guides and the rod's position should be noted before any change is made, and the exact position of the fly determined if that is possible. At least a sighting line should be taken over the fish's position to mark on the farther shore. A salmon shows himself and is gone in a brief moment of time. Once he has returned to the depths and the waves of his rising have dissolved into the rest or drifted downstream, it is impossible to know at just what spot he broke the surface unless there was a nearby rock or a distinctive crease in the flowing surface by which to locate it.

Having marked the spot where the salmon rose, the fly should be made to approach it in the same way. Dropping a fly on the salmon's head with a second cast won't duplicate a retrieve in which it swam toward the fish from ten or twenty feet beyond. The next cast bringing the fly to the salmon should be identical with the one causing the original rise. Variations in presenting the fly can come later. When the salmon lies in a slow or steady flow there should be little difficulty in repeating a cast. If the flow is rough and turbulent, the vagaries of the current will take a fly on a variety of courses in retrieves from identical casts. It may take more than a dozen identical casts (plus any that strayed from the pattern) to produce an exact repetition of the fly's presentation to the fish. This calls for continued casting, with the particular cast that rose the fish in mind, for a fair length of time.

It is easy to see how little chance a careless anger who simply casts his fly in the general direction of the salmon has of duplicating a given presentation in a turbulent flow. Strict attention to such details in fishing often means the difference between catching a salmon that has been risen once and failing to interest him again. It can mean the difference between reporting two rises and no fish in the day's log or reporting two fine salmon.

At the Portland Creek camps the guides were universally agreed in reporting that, almost without exception, when their charges rose a salmon, they would automatically strip out another few feet of line and continue their casting with the new and greater length of line. Apparently there is something about the salmon's rise to a fly to indicate that he has to come forward to take it. The angler therefore lengthens the line to bring the fly a little closer to the fish in order to make it just a little easier for him to reach it. They cling to this new casting distance stubbornly, failing to realize that although they may have made it easier for the salmon to get to the fly they cannot, with the longer cast, rekindle the situation that sparked his rise in the first place.

After a missed rise, even when there are a group of salmon concentrated in a small area, the salmon angler is still fishing for one particular fish that, at that time, may be the only one of them at all susceptible to his particular fly and method of fishing it. Having drawn one rise, he has a much greater chance of rerising that particular fish than of drawing a rise from another . . . except where conditions for the taking of salmon are particularly good.

When water drops to summer level, a salmon fisherman is somewhat akin to a hunter who stalks a particular buck. It is one of the things that makes salmon fishing the unusual sport it is. There is a great thrill to the moment when a salmon rises short to the fly and the fisherman plants his feet firmly on the streambed, bracing against the flow, and says to himself, hopefully, "Here we go again, *Salar. En garde!*"

[1957]

CHAPTER NINE

THE WONDERFUL POOL

*B*y the time this chapter was first published, in 1959,
Wulff had gotten his pilot's license and had been exploring La-
brador for a number of years with his float-equipped Piper Cub.
I've never been really sure whether this was brave, stupid, or—
as he assured me—really quite safe. I do know that he spent
many seasons flying alone through some of the wildest country
imaginable and was often the first sportsman to cast a fly on
many of the waters he visited. There was no way to get to most
of these places except by air, of course, and in so doing I know
he sampled and learned from what was the most untouched
salmon fishing in the world. Such fishing exists no longer. While
some salmon populations are recovering from damage done to

them in recent years, the wilderness itself—while still wild in many areas—is increasingly well traveled.

\--------

PICKING THE SITE for a Labrador salmon-fishing camp should have been the most pleasant of jobs. Instead, it had become a work of desperation for the three of us. August was already half gone, but snow patches still dotted the inland hills. The wind, though not strong, drifted cold from the iceberg-laden sea, and the rivers hadn't yet settled down to their early summer level.

Worst of all, the salmon—due back in the rivers weeks before from their feeding travels in the Atlantic—either hadn't yet arrived or were so widely scattered in the full streams that up to now it had been impossible to make an accurate estimate of fishing possibilities.

Something else that made us apprehensive was the knowledge that another group was in the area looking for the ideal spot to establish a salmon-fishing camp. We both sought a special river, or section of a river, where Atlantic salmon would congregate for a while as they worked toward its headwaters. We hoped to find some closely grouped pools that would provide a three-week period of fishing for a dozen anglers. The first one to find and occupy such an area could "stake it out." No one else would be likely to build beside it any more than we'd encroach on the two camps built on the best two of the known rivers. Legally, of course, we might locate near them, but an unwritten law dictated that we find our own spot.

None of the few well-known rivers in Labrador was either good enough or accessible enough. So our hopes lay in one of the many rivers, large and small, that had been neither fished nor studied by anglers. No one knew if these rivers roared over falls impassable for salmon or flowed smoothly from source to sea, whether they held suitable spawning grounds and good fishing pools or whether they were accessible by air.

We had a few sketchy reports, but we found falls where they

weren't supposed to be and young salmon above supposedly impassable falls. In more than 500 miles of coastline, less than a dozen rivers had been fished, and time was moving on.

In a float-equipped Beaver aircraft, we'd ranged from the Strait of Belle Isle, off the southeast tip of Labrador, to the rivers north of Hopedale. The plane now rested in the salt water near the mouth of the newest river we had to explore. Robin Jones, the pilot, had stayed with the plane, moving it to keep it afloat as the tide left the gravelly beach. He'd slipped on the mossy rocks as we came to shore and had taken a ducking. We could picture him crouched over a one-burner stove in some leafy shelter brewing coffee, or in the aircraft's cabin, damply avoiding the wind.

An officer of the Royal Canadian Mounted Police, 150 miles away, had told us that salmon should now be in this river, though the lone commercial salmon netter who operated in the nearby salt water reported a very disappointing catch.

Just below me, Dave Burchinal stood waist-deep in the clear, cold water and cast toward the center of the stream. He'd seen a salmon roll and was methodically dropping his fly to the waves, watching the current sweep it away in a swift arc. When the water dropped this would be a pool—a good resting place for salmon. But now the water seemed too fast for effective fishing.

On the bank behind me lay two grilse. These one-year, sea-feeding salmon of about five pounds had boiled up out of the eddies to take a fly and had eventually been captured after exhausting themselves in frantic runs and leaps. But two such small salmon, when taken from an unfished pool, aren't much of a promise of good fishing. If a salmon pool is to provide good fishing for several men for a number of weeks, it must show signs of many fish. The first cream-scooping angler to reach it should have fishing of a sort he'd never forget.

A light rain pelted its endless pattern on the water and against our faces. Low scud swept by as the sky darkened. Dave, tiring of his unrewarding casting, waved and shouted that he was going to fish his way down toward the plane.

"Don't you want to go up to the falls?" I shouted, but he shook his head and started downstream. It was 6 P.M.

We'd seen a pair of low waterfalls from the airplane before we landed. Foam and white water swept through the pools below them, and they didn't offer much promise. We'd come this far, though, and since any falls is likely to cause a salmon concentration when the run is on, I decided to hike on up the remaining half a mile and make sure this wasn't the river we were searching for.

Bushes clawed at my rainjacket and waders, threatening to rip them. Slippery rocks were ready to send my feet skidding out from under me. When the bushes were too thick or the banks too sheer for any progress except by wading, the powerful flow sought to pour in over the tops of my waders. It was 6:30 when I scaled the last rock barricade and stood at the tail of the basin that lay between the upper and lower falls.

I saw where the river hit the upper falls and plunged into the pool about eighty yards upstream. Then it swept through the pool and—just to the left of the rock where I now stood—dived over a lip of rock and formed the lower falls. Along the left side of the pool the river ran past a rock wall that jutted straight up. As I looked to the right, however, I saw the river boiling up in a semicircular eddy where the wind joined with surging currents to create a rough and endlessly changing pattern. In the dim light, I looked into the water close to the rock I stood on and thought I saw the flash of a grilse moving away.

As my eyes became accustomed to the faint light, I could see the nearby bottom during moments when foam and waves were at their minimum. A salmon swam by—a good one. I began moving to the right around the rock basin, working my way toward the white water that poured in at the far end of the great semicircle. I stepped out on a rocky point jutting into the pool.

Now I could see fish plainly. Two swam by. Then three, the far fish almost invisible under the dark, rain-flecked waves. I felt hard knots in my stomach. A fish went by every few seconds— all big salmon, fish that would weigh twenty to thirty pounds and more. After the long weeks of searching, this was like a beautiful dream. My grip tightened on the slender bamboo rod. With numbed fingers I loosed the fly from under the rubber band circling my rod grip, and pulled some slack from the reel. Methodically I broke off the three feet of five-pound-test tippet and a foot or more of the tapering leader above it. Eight-pound strength would be none too strong for salmon such as these. I retied the #6 low-water fly that had taken the grilse and made a cast.

The fly swam beneath the surface chop, alternately visible and invisible. The gray-green shapes moved past on their restless courses, but none showed the slightest deviation toward my fly. Rain still pelted down and the sky was darker. My watch showed 6:50 P.M.—time to go. Instead, I moved farther around the basin.

Another point jutted out. The water beneath it was deep and dark, and there, too, I saw salmon. Knowing the Atlantic salmon's built-in resistance to flies or lures, even when he's freshly in from the sea and has never seen an artificial fly, I was looking for a steady current where these restless fish would hang motionless above the bottom in an easy flow. Then I could cast again and again to the same fish. Here, where the fish were constantly on the move, only coincidence would put the fly just ahead of a salmon at a moment when he might boil over and take it. I eased around the shoreline, working my way through some alders and low spruce.

When I reached the water's edge again, it was where the eddy met the incoming flow. Amid the surface waves beside the white water there was one patch, perhaps twenty-five feet across, clearer than the rest. There, lying in formation, were fifteen or twenty very large salmon, especially impressive after the other Labrador rivers where almost all the fish are in the four- to six-pound category.

Quietly I stripped line off the reel and made a cast. The fly swung slowly over the school. I thought one moved a little higher as the fly passed. Next cast the fly dropped just ahead of him, and I drew it slowly toward shore. For a moment the salmon was impassive, then swam lazily behind the fly. I slowed the retrieve, and still the fish was scarcely gaining. Trying to maintain some motion in the fly, I finally drew it in against the rocks. The fish was still following, and its jaws opened.

It was a fish of more than twenty-five pounds, with a small head and a long, sleek, heavy body. His lazy motion brought him almost to my feet where the fly was brushing against the stone. The gills flared, and then the jaws clamped tight—a fraction of an inch behind the feathers. Slowly the salmon turned with a flash of his silvery belly and returned to the others.

Mechanically I cast that wet fly over and over again, straining my eyes to watch it and to watch the fish as well—when I could see them under the waves and the raindrop patterns. The fish were never really still. They were working slowly up through that bit of current, then suddenly they'd be gone, only to reappear at the tail of the eddy and slowly work up through the current again.

Down at the plane they were impatient, I knew. We had planned to take off by 7:30 at the latest. If we delayed till 8:00, we'd barely have time to reach the river settlement of Postville, forty-odd miles away, and moor the ship before full darkness.

I drew out a large, low-water fly, a #1, which I'd fashioned something like a Jock Scott, and threw a riffling hitch—a couple of half hitches just behind the head. This arrangement makes the fly ride the surface like an aquaplane, the head and eye high, with a rippling V-wake spreading out behind. On retrieve after retrieve, it swung across the school of salmon.

One of the largest, with a white scar near his dorsal fin, seemed more restless than the others. Eventually I saw him lift a little when the fly passed over. The fish were quite close to me and almost ready to drop out of sight to reappear below me at the eddy's foaming tail. Another cast—perhaps two—were possible before they moved away, and when next they worked their way up, that big salmon's restlessness might have passed.

When the fly touched water and started its swing, the big salmon lifted easily beneath it. He rose slowly, showing the pearly white of his underjaw, before he broke the surface and engulfed the fly. My light rod lifted sharply, and I felt solid resistance. I held the rod high and took in line as the salmon wrenched his body on the surface. Again his head broke through to air. His mouth opened convulsively, and the fly, hardly fifteen feet from me, whipped back past my ear.

The fish was gone and so was the time—7:20. If I hooked a fish now, even if it took less than half an hour to play it, we would be late. Such a delay would mean a dangerous flight or a damp, cold night in the cramped plane cabin.

Still nursing a recently sprained ankle, I made the best possible time down the river. I picked up my two grilse beside the lower pool, grateful that the bear we'd seen from the air hadn't found them. Weary and out of breath, I crunched along the gravel beach toward the cold and tired men at the plane. I realized now it was best that I'd failed to hook the salmon. Had I played him, we'd never have had time to make our flight.

Though some of the salmon might climb the falls during the night, there'd be nearly as many there tomorrow, even if no new ones moved in from below. Surely a morning's fishing would bring some action.

As I laid the grilse down on the float, Dave looked at me and said, "Look, Robin, he's got a strange light in his eyes."

"Fish like these are only minnows where I've just been," I said. "We've got a date with a thirty-pounder tomorrow."

They were ready to leave. I told them the story as we flew, and plans were reshuffled to give us the morning at the wonderful pool.

The low clouds passed with the night. And when the three of us reached the river the following morning, the sun shone between bright puffs of cumulus clouds. With an incoming tide, our moored plane would stay afloat without attention.

All three of us passed the lower pools and went directly to the spot where I'd ended up the night before. Under the bright sun the cruising salmon were readily visible. There seemed to be even more than I remembered. We saw one leap the falls above the pool, traveling ten feet in the air before disappearing into foam. We rigged up.

A salmon took Dave's fly and cartwheeled across the eddy into the swift run that swept along the rock face on the pool's left side. There the fish turned downstream, and the reel piped a high crescendo. Dave's line poured out, then the backing went too. There was no slackening of the reel's whine, and we knew what would happen. Even though the fish might break free at the leader, which was designed to break before the line, the current's powerful drag on the fly line—which had been carried down into the roaring water far below us—would increase the backing's strain to well above the leader's. The backing parted at the splice where it joined the fly line. Fortunately we had another line.

Dave's second fish circled the eddy. That wide sweep bellied the line far out, and when the salmon leaped near the rocks at the tail of the pool, the line snagged. In a wild scramble over the rocky shore, Dave freed it. Soon the salmon was deep in a slow flow close by. Next the fish ran up into the white water, and from there the episode with the first fish was repeated at the cost of another line, leader and fly.

From then on, Dave fished with only the fine backing line that was left on his reel. Casting was most difficult, and no more salmon rose, but two fine trout came out of a small eddy against the rocks.

My salmon finally came up to a high-floating, white dry fly as big as a butterfly. I played him gently as a trout, letting my rod (entire scale weight two ounces) bend but lightly, trying to avoid any harsh pressure that would send him off on any wild and frantic rush. He moved to the middle of the pool then rejoined the others at the tail of the eddy where I'd hooked him. Leaving them, he bored down with increasing strength into the big hole where the eddy was sucked back into the main flow. I perched on the rock ledge above him, knee-deep in waves. After about ten minutes, when some of his strength and wildness were gone, he tried a run across the pool. He did it at such reduced speed that I could follow around the shore and, when the run was over, slowly work him back.

Standing behind me on the rocky ledge, Robin was busily recording events with a movie camera. He took pictures for nearly half an hour before the great fish began to tire. Snapped on at my back I had a salmon-tailer, a snaring device that nooses a played-out salmon by the tail and lets you lift him ashore. I was reaching for the salmon-tailer when Robin said, "Why don't you pick him up bare-handed like you do the grilse. It'll make a better picture."

He was right about the picture. But this was the biggest fish I could hope to catch all season, and hand-tailing is a tricky deal. Finally I dropped my arm and slid my sleeve up a little.

The fish came by, close enough but in the wrong position. I could have had him with the tailer, but without it I had to wait. He moved down under the ledge. Half a minute went by before I could bring him in again. Again I dared not risk trying to grip him, for if I touched him and missed, he'd pull away and be tougher to bring in close.

When the curving rod swung him past a third time, he headed in against the rocks and rested there a moment—still strong but weary. While the tackle held his head up lightly, I reached deep and found the grip I wanted at his tail. I closed my hand and lifted him in the paralyzing tail grip—forty-one inches of bright Atlantic salmon.

He must have weighed nearly thirty pounds. We'll never know, however, for when we left that wonderful pool we traveled north and then back south again. Before we reached scales that could weigh him, the fish was eaten.

After all our further searchings were over, we went back to the wonderful pool and made our plans. The camp was under construction by the time the salmon had moved on to the upper water. But spring will come again—then summer which, in Labrador, is like our spring. The salmon will climb once more to that pool and tarry there. And so, if fortune wills, will I.

Our explorations were confidential, so I can't reveal the exact location of the pool or the river in which it lies. But I can guarantee that sportsmen with the will and means to reach the unfished Labrador areas when the salmon are in from the sea will find adventure. They may even find for themselves a still more wonderful pool, as yet unknown to any angler.

[1959]

CHAPTER TEN

A WORD OF ADVICE
FOR THE NOVICE

*I*t is difficult in many ways for the trout fisherman to
go salmon fishing, because the fishing is at once superficially
similar yet dramatically different. Most new salmon fishermen,
however, are making the transition from trout fishing, and for
most of these the advice in this and subsequent chapters is in-
valuable.

••••••••

FISHING FOR BRIGHT ATLANTIC SALMON is not like fishing for other
fish, for the salmon rarely, if ever, feeds on anything in the rivers.
Nature nauseates the salmon when they return from the sea to
their native rivers on their spawning runs. In fresh water again

they are like a man with a severe hangover who has either lost the desire for food or, if he does attempt eating, finds he cannot keep even the first mouthful down. He cannot be tempted through the hunger that is the downfall of most fish taken by angling.

The only legal way of angling for Atlantic salmon in North America is by fly-fishing, and the small fly is thought by many to be a torment rather than a tidbit. It is small and inconspicuous, almost always fished near the surface and in moving water. There is a great deal of water to cover, and the fly must usually be placed close to the salmon to be effective. The first mistake beginners usually make is to fish most of their time over water that is barren of fish where salmon can neither see nor react to their flies.

An experienced angler who knows a pool well will realize just where the salmon tend to lie and rest. He will fish those spots, and his fly will be passing just in front of the resting salmon in cast after cast, hour after hour. The novice who hasn't the knowledge of where salmon are lying in the pool usually covers all the seemingly good water and will have his fly passing near salmon only ten percent or so of the time. Obviously, the angler who knows the pool in this case has at least ten times as much chance of catching a salmon as one who does not. A suggested remedy for the novice is to fish for at least fifty percent of the time over spots where he has seen salmon jump or where for any other reason he is sure salmon are lying. The surest remedy is to hire a guide who knows the waters thoroughly and follow his advice. Salmon move from one resting spot in a pool to another when the water level rises or falls, and only experience can teach where salmon will lie under a particular water condition in a given river.

A second major fault of the novice is his failure to watch his fly intently and continuously. Whether fishing wet fly or dry the angler should always watch his fly and the water under and around it. The angler who does and who notices the slightest flash of silver or other sign of a salmon moving beneath it and who then stops to fish for cast after cast to that spot will usually hook or catch that fish. This may happen several times in a fishing day and result in his taking several salmon while the angler who has not been watching his fly intently and who therefore failed to concentrate on catching these interested but inconspicuous fish takes none at all.

Salmon often take a little coaxing to get them to rise. The first cast over them does not always bring them up to the full effort of taking the fly. Changing the fly may be the answer, but more often than not it is something else, a certain path it follows or a certain speed and direction of the fly at a certain point. Of a hundred casts over a salmon, only one or two follow the particular path and speed that will cause him to take the fly. How to achieve the right fly path and speed of travel for a wet fly over a salmon is not easy to explain, but to understand that such a need exists and that the hundredth unsuccessful cast to the same spot may be followed by one that hooks a salmon is a long step forward in becoming an accomplished salmon fisherman.

Once a salmon takes a fly most novices hold him too hard; the greatest percentage of salmon hooked and lost are lost in the first few seconds or minute of play and for that reason. The salmon should be allowed free rein for a period of several minutes before the angler tries to put any serious tackle pressure upon him. Tackle pull should be used only after some of the wildness is out of the salmon, and his runs are more readily predictable and more easily cushioned by the rod.

In playing a salmon, the habit of some trout fishermen of playing their fish by stripping line instead of working the line directly from the reel usually ends in a disaster. A salmon is too fast and too strong a fish to be handled readily with coils of loose line in danger of tangling between the reel and first guide. And an automatic reel is not suitable equipment for salmon fishing. Automatics do not have the necessary line and rewind capacities in proportion to their weight. When a fish runs fast and far against an automatic reel, the playing pressure at the reel builds up instead of being relaxed as a good fisherman with a standard reel prefers it.

At the end of a fight the tired salmon should not be forced. He is too big to "hold" with normal tackle and must be led into a landing position by skill rather than force no matter how weary he seems to be. Salmon are famous for that last bit of reserve strength and a final unexpected rush or leap that wins freedom for them.

If a fish is hurried in the final moment and is missed by the net, tailer or gaff, he will be doubly hard to bring into good landing position again. Advice for the novice is to be particularly sure your fish is ready for landing before attempting it and to exercise extreme caution once you have tried and failed.

[1960]

CHAPTER ELEVEN

COMMON FAULTS OF A SALMON ANGLER

*I*t sometimes seems that half the battle in salmon fishing is casting your fly in the right place at the right time. A good salmon guide, of course, will know that salmon have held three feet this side of that white rock at this water level during every season of his guiding life, for example, and that makes things relatively simple. Salmon and trout typically hold in different spots and for different reasons, which is yet another of the things about salmon fishing that confounds most trout fishermen. This 1961 chapter offers some basic help for the salmon angler on his own.

IT TAKES LONG EXPERIENCE to know precisely where salmon will lie in any given river under a specific water condition. However, there are general rules to follow, and every salmon angler should know them. The Atlantic salmon is a restless fish, torn between a desire to use and enjoy his remarkable stored-up energy, which may give rise to his periodic leaping, and the need to conserve that energy, for he will gain no more through feeding or in any other way. The long ordeal of river travel and spawning lie just ahead.

So he will choose a slow current or an eddy to lie in where a slow flow soothes his restlessness. The positions or "lies" normally stretch from the point in the pools where the inrushing current slows down enough to lose the extreme turbulence of its entry on down through the length of the pool to its tail. Salmon do not scatter themselves casually but select only certain spots that please them. And as the flow slows down from spring to summer some salmon will move closer to the heads of the pools. Others, resting in a pool, will change their lies or move on with a raising or lowering of as little as an inch of water level.

Salmon often lie at the edges of the current, near or upon the shallow bars, and close to shore. Those greener pastures well out in the middle of the river or near the far shore may not hold half as many salmon as the shallow waters of the shore from which you fish. Salmon tend to take a fly more readily in shallow water than in deep, another factor to keep in mind. Wading through the good salmon lies near the shore without fishing them carefully first is a very common fault among beginning salmon anglers.

The perfect wet-fly cast for most conditions is one in which the line straightens out completely as it falls to the water at a downstream angle of approximately forty-five degrees. If the line does not straighten out all the way, the fisherman not only loses the farthest and often the best part of the fly's retrieve while waiting for the fly to come under proper tension and follow the line as the current swings it down and across the stream, but also a little fishing time is lost with this wait in each slack cast. Such a minor loss of time before the poorly cast fly is fishing correctly may not seem important at first glance, but time during which a wet fly just sits still in the water, like time spent in false casting, is wasted in terms of catching fish; many wasted moments added together may make up just the extra time needed to turn a blank day into a successful one.

As the wet fly swings with the current it may be necessary to mend the line by a partly-completed roll cast to one side or the other. It may be wise to lift the rod tip to speed up the fly's pace or to lower the tip to slow it down as it crosses a particularly fast bit of current. These are the niceties of fishing the wet fly to be worked out *after* the perfect, straight-out cast has become a habit.

When the Portland Creek hitch is used and the wet fly is skimmed across the surface on the retrieve, the necessity of a good, straight cast is increased, since if the fly sinks far (on slack) after it lands some extra time is required for it to plane up to the surface to reach the right fishing position.

Bad casts are made occasionally by all anglers. If one lands in the water and there are or may be fish beneath it, the smart thing to do is to tighten up the line quickly and fish the bad cast through for whatever distance it affords. The worst thing to do is to snatch it back into the air, disturbing the surface with a fish-frightening commotion. No other angling fault so clearly denotes the bumbler as compounding his error in this manner because he is too lazy to use his left hand, take in the slack line and fish through to a normal pick-up point. Although one always aims for perfection in every cast of the day, the bad cast, made occasionally and fished through, instead of putting a salmon off may make just the swing that causes him to rise.

As long as there is a possibility in the angler's mind that his fly is still in good salmon water, he should fish the cast through till the line straightens out below him. Extending the time on each cast during which the fly travels properly through good fishing water increases the percentage of real fishing time in proportion to "dead time" (casting, changing flies, motionless fly, etc.).

The angle of the cast to the current has a bearing, too, on the time a fly fishes in each cast. The nearer the cast is to straight downstream the less time and shorter distance per cast the fly will swim. As the angle with the downstream flow is increased, the time of the sweep is increased, but the angle grows bad beyond forty-five degrees and the fly may become (1) less attractive to the salmon and (2) so fast in its travel that it will be missed if a fish does rise.

The wet-fly rise depends upon many things—the speed of the water, the mood of the fish and the fish's accuracy are among them. Salmon miss flies through error. They also miss them on purpose, passing close as if to frighten them or just to practice. Regardless of the reason for the rise, a fish that has risen and failed to connect is more likely to rise again than is another fish beside him, which has not yet been stirred to make a move toward the fly. The common fault involved when a rise is missed is a failure to fix immediately in mind the exact length of line out at the moment of that rise in order that future casts and retrieves can duplicate the one that moved the fish. More often than not the angler has an illusion that the distance is greater than it actually was and tends to strip more line from the reel. As a result the following casts are longer, and on the retrieve the fly passes downstream of the path it took that first drew interest from the fish. Indications are strong that the identical cast is the best one to bring a fish back to the fly again.

Some anglers rest a fish after a missed rise. Others, who do not want to lose their ability to duplicate the cast by moving away or wasting time in inaction, cast back immediately, a system that is often successful. There can be no hard and fast rule here for not all salmon react the same way. Sometimes, apparently, it is wise to wait, and sometimes it is not. If a decision is made to cast back immediately, experience dictates that if a few good casts do not produce the desired rise a resting of the fish is indicated before working the spot over with a variety of flies.

To strike or not to strike when a salmon rises to a wet fly? *Do not strike! Do set the hook!* Any movement of the fly before the salmon gets it into his mouth is more likely to cause him to miss it than to help in hooking him. So, until he takes the fly into his mouth and causes a distinct pressure upon the line, the angler should not cause the fly to deviate from its appointed path. Setting the hook is something that may be accomplished automatically by the drag of the water on the line or by the movement of the fish. However, unless the hook is very small and sharp and the rise is deliberate and accurate, some pressure may be needed, not to start the point of the hook into the flesh but to drive the hook in beyond the barb. Such a lifting of the rod to sink the hook is advisable with large hooks or with doubles—or when the rise is awkward and the points may embed in tough gristle or bone.

No long-fishing angler will come out with a perfect record on hooked rises, but most will admit that it is better to deliver too little pressure too late than too much too soon. A wet fly is normally under enough tension and moving at sufficient speed to embed its point into the flesh. The salmon's movement and the current's tension on the line will usually do the rest. Hooking the dry-fly rise is quite another story—something to take up in the future.

[1961]

CHAPTER TWELVE

SALMON FISHING IN ICELAND

*T*his chapter is partly based on a fishing tour Wulff made of Icelandic salmon rivers in 1973, and those same rivers remain today as popular destinations for traveling anglers. Salmon management in Iceland is a good example of the fine fishing that can be produced by the realization of economic self-interest. Typically, riparian landowners here group together to market their salmon and salmon rivers primarily for sportfishing, which generates far more income per salmon caught than a commercial fishery. As a result, Icelandic salmon runs have held up in numbers over years when commercial overuse depressed salmon runs in Canada and in Europe.

THE ATLANTIC SALMON is generally conceded to be the king of the stream fish. Among the basic reasons are that he's taken on trout tackle and he's much bigger than trout are. He is tougher than trout because of both his sea experience, which gives him a sense of space and distance, and his great store of energy. He doesn't feed while in the stream, as a trout does, and has built up a store of energy a trout doesn't need . . . and doesn't have. The small hooks and fine leaders of the flies he takes call for more skill and make landing him more difficult, more challenging. Fly-fishing is the only legal method of Atlantic-salmon angling in the United States and Canada, and the "fly only" restriction is growing in European rivers.

Atlantic salmon are a sadly diminished and still diminishing species. They still suffer from heavy commercial takes in the sea. They suffer, too, from bad biological management such as the forcing by law of a net-mesh size that ensures the taking of the big fish, the best breeding stock, while allowing free passage of the runts to the spawning ground.

The great American salmon rivers were lost, primarily, to dams. The Canadian rivers were mismanaged and poorly protected. The British rivers went down to low numbers on several occasions and were built back by very good management. Now salmon populations suffer from indiscriminate high seas fishing with drift nets, which are, we hope, being phased out.

Norway's rivers were not as well managed or controlled as the British rivers and they, too, have suffered heavily from the high seas fishery. Norway, perhaps, had the finest fishing of all and, in recent years, the biggest fish. Anglers have paid as much as $5,000 per week, per fisherman, to fish one of Norway's "fly fishing only" rivers. But with the salmon decline Norway's fishing is no longer the best available. That honor can now be claimed by Iceland, where, by a combination of good fortune and good management, they offer the world's best Atlantic salmon fishing.

Their fish have not been pillaged in the sea because the feeding grounds of the Icelandic salmon still remains their own secret. At home the Icelanders managed well, using angling and fly fishing as their major harvesting method. Anglers have always been willing to pay more for salmon than have commercial net-ting groups, so a well-regulated, strictly limited catch for Iceland has brought a far greater monetary return for a smaller per-centage of their salmon run—building the runs up instead of tearing them down.

Today the Iceland rivers still run clear and clean with salmon runs at near-maximum capacity. The season runs from early June till early September, and the "beats" are designed to make each day's angling not only challenging but fully rewarding.

As in the rest of Europe the salmon rivers are under private ownership and control. Because of this they have all had far better management than our American rivers have had. Every owner tries to pass on to his grandchildren a river of greater value and productivity than he received. Our rivers are not man-aged by people who suffer financially if they are mismanaged. Our unborn grandchildren do not vote. So we in America have our democracy; they in Europe have superior fishing, which is why Americans must travel to a foreign country to get good salmon fishing—and pay what it's worth.

Three rivers, in particular, stand out in Iceland. The first is the Grimsa, located a two-hour drive westward from Reykjavik, the country's capital and its largest city. Accommodations are at a newly completed fishing lodge designed by famed salmon an-gler and author Ernest Schwiebert. The lodge looks out on a falls where, when conditions are right, one can see salmon of from four to thirty pounds hurtling out of the foam at the base into the falling water that leads on up to their spawning areas.

The Grimsa flows for forty miles through a meadowed valley, and except for a short stretch near the falls, it flows at an easy pace. In its many "classic" pools of good fly-taking water the angler will find easy casting and slow and easy currents that will help make his fly look attractive to the salmon. He'll find that his salmon has plenty of room in which to run and there'll be quiet water, conveniently located, in which to bring his tired fish to the guide's net or hand to complete the capture.

The tackle used now is typical of the changing world of

Atlantic-salmon angling. Most anglers use typical trout rods of from eight to nine feet long, and ranging in weight from five to six-and-a-half ounces. A few use detachable butts on their trout-type rods, and a few still use the longer (up to twelve-and-a-half feet) rods of yesterday's salmon angler. A small group, too, go to even lighter gear. For instance, I use a six-foot, one-piece, 1.67-ounce fiberglass fly rod of my own design (Garcia No. 2070). My wife and I both used these ultra light salmon rods during our 1973 Iceland trip in spite of a few windy days. Joan finds the light rods delightful and less tiring. For me they offer the greatest challenge.

A long-bellied, forward-taper fly line gives the greatest combination of delicacy and accuracy in casting, combined with maximum distance and the time-saving longer pickup with a preliminary roll. We like a white line so we can see better where the fly will travel and the speed of its movement.

The reel should be the lightest, well-made, single-action reel that will hold the fly line and up to two hundred yards of backing that an angler needs on Iceland's salmon rivers. The heavier multiplying reels work well on two-handed fly rods, but are much too heavy for single-handed fly casting.

Leaders matched closely to the line diameter at the butt should taper down to the angler's choice of from five to fifteen pounds at the tippet, depending on fly size, river conditions and the angler's skill.

The flies used in Iceland are, for the most part, the traditional type of fly the British brought with them when they opened up the Icelandic fly fishing over a hundred years ago. Give the guides a look at your fly box, and they'll search for patterns like Black Doctor, Jock Scott, Silver Gray, Black Dose, Wilkinson, Blue Charm and others similarly time honored. Other wet flies will work, of course, but most guides and most salmon anglers tend to stick to the patterns and sizes they've caught salmon with before.

Dry flies do not work to any large degree in Iceland, perhaps because of the lack of fly hatches in their rivers or the cooler water temperatures. Icelandic salmon *will* take a dry fly, but they prefer a wet fly by a margin of at least ten to one.

You'll need some cold-weather clothing for Iceland for, even in the summer, a seventy-degree day may be followed by a "freezer" when the wind from the northern seas whistles in and makes some anglers bundle up with down undergarments and outer shells that shed the rain and break the wind. Generally Iceland's climate is like May in Maine.

Chest waders with felt soles are the best equipment. There is no boat fishing on the Grimsa, although some of the other rivers require boats to fish some of the larger, deeper pools.

Fishing in Iceland is normally a morning and evening endeavor. The rivers are open from 7 A.M. to 1 P.M and from 4 P.M. to 10 P.M. We found about nine hours a day to be quite satisfying. It gave us more than enough time to enjoy the fine meals and accommodations and a little salmon fishing conversation with our companions on the rivers. The Grimsa has sixty-five pools divided into five beats and takes a complement of ten anglers at one time, with two anglers sharing each beat.

The Nordura, close to the Grimsa, is a river of approximately the same size that joins it and others to empty into the sea. However, it is far different in character. It flows through rough, volcanic country at a swifter speed. It has more white water with more fragmented rock and less gravel underfoot. The scenery is dramatic, and each pool has a background of rising cliffs and steep slopes. The salmon of the Nordura are slimmer and more trim. One cannot say that they fight harder than the Grimsa salmon, but in the faster, rough water, they present a greater tackle problem.

The lodge at the Nordura looks up the beautiful valley to the falls, a white-water setting for a beautiful pool below it. There are ten pools and five beats on the Nordura and two anglers share each beat.

The queen of the Icelandic rivers is the Laxa i Adaldal, which flows north and is located on the northwestern shore of the island. You'll fly over glaciers to reach it and find it lying in a broad, gently sloping valley. There is a power dam and a lake above the salmon fishing water on the Laxa, which makes it unique among salmon rivers—a stream with a controlled flow. There are no floods, no drouths, for this river. The springs, some of them warm, keep the river temperature within the range the salmon love best.

The salmon of the Laxa run larger than those of the Grimsa and Nordura. A number of fish of more than thirty pounds are taken every year. The average size for salmon on the Laxa is over thirteen pounds.

A few of the Laxa's best pools are quite large and deep and require a boat for their fishing. Your guide will take you in a stubby river boat of special Icelandic design and row you to the best casting positions. He may move you slowly with easy strokes, or he may anchor and let you fish one "drop" after another until you've covered the productive water. The pools are quite accessible by car and very little walking is required to reach the fishing; whereas on the Nordura and the Grimsa there are quarter-mile trails to traverse and meadows to walk across.

The Laxa has a considerable weed growth due to the constant level of the flow of its rich, clear waters. These weeds can cause problems at certain times during the season when their growth is at maximum and the wind and waves churn the water to break off drifting lengths of weed. However, this is considered a small price to pay for a chance to catch its big fish and walk or wade along its constant-level banks.

The lodge at the Laxa, like the others, is modern and comfortable. There's a sauna to revitalize the weary casting muscles and the food will delight any traveler—early, late and often. The trip by air from Reykjavik is an interesting experience, and the traveler looks down not only on glaciers, but also on silvery rivers and lakes and mountains that reach up some six thousand feet from sea level.

The Icelandic people are thoughtful, charming hosts, warm and friendly. Altogether the combination of their hospitality and the world's best salmon angling makes a trip to their country a unique and wonderful angling experience.

The Icelandic rivers are well managed, and the take is well

within a safe harvest. Five fish you catch are yours to take home, to have smoked if you wish; the rest remain the property of the farmer, but special arrangements can be made if you want to take more than five home. There is no need to release salmon in this well-managed fishery, but we released twenty to put a little Darwinian pressure on the species. What if they overcrowd the river and they, or a similar number, don't make it and die? As Darwin brought out, under the pressure of competition the better, or more suited, survive; the weaker perish. If we did not help with more fish, we did, at least, give an impetus toward *better* salmon—if you believe that Icelandic salmon can be improved!

[1974]

CHAPTER THIRTEEN

Fair Hooks and Foul

*U*nder certain and sometimes common conditions of low water, it's relatively easy to deliberately foul-hook a salmon. "Foul" is also something of an understatement; there's nothing at all sporting about the act or the idea. It does happen, however, on almost all salmon rivers sometimes, especially when low water and warm weather make the salmon dour and reluctant to move to the best-fished fly. Wulff often advocated a single-hook rule, which would eliminate the sometimes popular double-hooked flies that make foul-hooking relatively easy. He long maintained that a single hook will fair-catch a salmon just as effectively as a double, making doubles unnecessary in spite of their long tradition of use.

———

- - - - - - - - -

THE FIRST TIME I saw a salmon "jigged" was back in 1933 on the Margaree. Very early in the morning, with waders on and tackle in hand, I'd left my tent in the field near the country hotel and walked to the bridge that crossed the river. As I neared the bridge, I saw a man on it with a long fly rod. He lifted the rod sharply and was fast to a salmon.

The river was twenty-five feet or more below the level of the steel truss, too high to jump down, too far to work the rod back to the end and down the steep grassy slope to the river beach. The angler simply dropped his rod from the bridge to splash in the shallow water below and raced for the bridge's end. I could hear the click of the big Uniqua reel, underwater, giving the subdued song of a fast-running fish. The man scurried to the end of the bridge and flashed down the steep, grassy bank, plunged into the shallows, retrieved the rod and resumed the playing of the salmon.

I walked to the high bank and watched. The salmon was hooked in the side, and when the angler lifted him toward the surface he showed widely silver, bright in the sun. I took out my pocket camera and took a picture.

The salmon was a twenty-five pounder, a female. When she lay shining on the beach, I walked down to take a look. She was beautiful—and there was just the smallest scar where the hook had torn the scales and held her. The fisherman, a small, wiry man with incredibly blue twinkling eyes, had noted my camera. Caught in the act, he wanted to make friends.

He said his name was Jim. I was a new visitor wasn't I? Camping in the field by the lodge?

Knowing I was new to the valley and couldn't afford a guide (few young anglers could in those Depression days), he looked at me quizzically and said, "I could take a day and show you all the pools in the river."

I hesitated a moment, then said, "That would be great!" I'd caught my first salmon on a dry fly the day before, but I didn't know the river. I knew it would save me a lot of learning time.

Without another word he knew I wouldn't report him to the guardian, and I knew I'd found someone who'd really show me where the fish were.

Jim was one of the best fishermen on the river but perhaps he loved to fish too much—and work too little. He was poor and, in the eyes of others, I was to learn, "shiftless." He could catch salmon with a fly as well as any other Margaree angler, but he just couldn't stand to leave those big fish lying there just because they wouldn't take a fly, if the time was right and no one would be the wiser.

To keep up the pretense of being an honorable angler, he held his "catches" to moderate limits. He explained that he'd once taken four fine fish out of the Hut pool in a single afternoon, hooking them fair and square but without fellow anglers to witness it. He'd pondered a while and hidden three in the bushes, taking them all home one at a time by devious ways. He knew that such a good catch would only cement in the minds of others the certainty that he had "stolen" them. He had learned to use extremely sharp hooks, doubles, of course, and even to take a salmon's own scales and, with slime, scale over the wounds he made. The veteran anglers of that river would never have overlooked what I, as a stranger, did not wish to become involved in. They'd have informed the warden because that time Jim had a sinker near the fly.

Later that day, as we walked back up the river carrying a sixteen-pounder Jim had caught properly with a Blue Charm, Duncan McKenzie, rodmaker and dean of the local guides, called out, "Did you take that one fair, Jim?"

Those early guides and anglers were, by and large, great sportsmen, and they held Jim in contempt and didn't hesitate to show it. And among men who live or fish by a code of honor there will always be contempt for those too mean of heart to live up to it. Duncan, whom I learned to know and admire, was warning me that Jim was no sportsman and that if I followed his pattern I, too, would be a subject for scorn.

Snatching salmon is like a disease, a fixation that no salmon a man can see—even one he can't see but knows is lying in a certain spot under discolored water—has a right to escape him.

Foul-hooking salmon becomes a surreptitious thievery, a taking of something undeserved; an admission of failure as an angler, but an admission that one must hide from honorable anglers and hold within one's self. Both dishonorable and illegal, it must be clandestine, except for those brazen few who will say, "Those salmon are mine as much as anyone's else. Maybe I'm not rich enough to have all the flies and tackle it takes to catch them, but I mean to take them *as my right*, law or no law."

Except for these brazen few, an angler who foul-hooks a salmon he was unable to hook honorably must walk back to his group with his head held high, proud of his catch, with an explanation of the particular fly and the strategy that turned the trick. Sometimes the hook mark in the fish's side must be explained, and always a hook mark must be put in the mouth to support the travesty.

[1974]

CHAPTER FOURTEEN

LONG ROD, SHORT ROD

As a general case, the angler who uses conventional methods year in and year out learns relatively little. In contrast, Lee Wulff's persistence in using salmon rods as short as six feet long when his contemporaries were using rods almost twice that size taught him all sorts of things about fly casting, fighting fish and other aspects of fishing. The basic idea was to create an angling challenge and, by working through that challenge, to become a better fisherman.

Over the years, he gained a reputation for short-rod advocacy that extends even beyond his own beliefs in this area. "To me," he once said, "the little rod is a challenge," adding that he thought it was perfectly okay if I wanted to continue fishing with my nine-footers.

· · · · · · · · ·

DECIDING WHAT LENGTH ROD to use for Atlantic salmon is a very personal thing. Everything from twenty feet and more down to no rod at all has been used successfully; each rod offers certain advantages and creates certain disadvantages. Let's see what some of them are.

The rods more than twelve feet long are essentially for two-handed casting and those of nine-and-a-half feet and less are designed to be cast with one hand. Two-handed casting is no more difficult than casting with one hand, but the longer, heavier rods will be a bit more tiring to hold and handle. They are also more bulky to carry, although this, and their greater weight, is a very minor consideration.

Long rods cast a high line well above an angler's head. They will lift a line higher in the water for the fly retrieve. They can keep the line above subsurface obstructions that would catch a line that traveled more deeply in the stream. They give a greater opportunity to exert directional control when a salmon is being played and they give a long cushion of resilience before a fish can bring pressure to take line. They mend line easier and give better control of the path and the speed of the fly. There is great grace and beauty to long-rod casting. What more could one ask?

Nothing, really, except . . . for an individual angler, unless the angler is beaching his fish on a wide beach, the long rod won't let the fisherman bring the fish in close enough to reach him with a net, a tailer or his hand. And it takes more strength to cast the heavier lines that balance the longer, heavier rods and is more tiring.

The development that gave shorter rods a comparable capability with the old-style long ones was the development of forward-taper or shooting-head lines. They concentrated weight in a shorter length at the head of the fly-casting line and let the angler "shoot" line to give him greater distance. Short rods will give higher speeds and drive lighter lines for long distances. A trained light-rod caster can cast as far with a light six-foot rod as with a much heavier nine-footer.

Choice of rod is a personal thing. A long time ago at a New York Anglers' Club program someone in the audience asked me what length rod I used and why. The question of why took me by surprise, but I thought for a moment and then came up with an answer I've never seen any reason to change. First, I replied, I'm interested in the challenges of angling. I want to use tackle that requires skill to accomplish its purpose. I want the angling problems to keep me on my toes, and the light rods which demand the fastest reactions give those challenges to me. On the other hand, I do not want to use a rod so light that I start to make excuses and feel that any other angler has a tackle advantage in catching or playing fish that I cannot equal or overcome by sheer skill.

For me, this works out to a rod of about six feet and with bamboo or glass at a total weight of under an ounce-and-three-quarters. If I went to a lighter rod, I might be tempted to make excuses. When I went to Iceland to fish some years back, I was prepared to use a seven-and-a-half-foot rod because of the high winds. I was chided, "What's the matter with you? Isn't your six-foot rod big enough for these fish?" So I fished the entire time with the six-footer and was as successful, I am sure, as I could have been with any other rod.

Now for the advantages of the small rod. The first is that it casts with speed and doesn't call for hard work. I can cast all day and never feel the slightest fatigue. Second, it uses a line of fine diameter that offers little drag to the currents of the stream, a situation which allows me to use lighter leaders and smaller hooks successfully. Third, it lets me bring my fish in close where I can hand-tail them most easily. I have demonstrated this complete, "in-close" playing control many times by letting salmon pass between my legs, then passing the rod through behind them and continuing the play without interruption.

I do not recommend the ultralight rods for everyone. For the average angler, rods of eight-and-a-half to nine-and-a-half feet will give the greatest effectiveness with the minimum of skill and effort. If an angler wants to go lighter he will need to develop special skills and, through them, gain special rewards.

Small, light rods call for special techniques. In the long years of my using them, which started in the 1930s, I've changed my casting and fish-playing techniques drastically. Without those changes I could not make them as effective as I do. Casting them calls for increased speed, more arm movement and, ideally, an oval casting motion rather than the conventional figure-eight action.

I can, under ideal conditions, make casts of as much as ninety feet and feel comfortable when fishing in the sixty- to seventy-five-foot range. On windy days I can make up, with sheer speed, for the problem of wind penetration and control as well as with the long rods. With my ultralight rods I feel very close to my salmon when I play them. I can feel their movements and sense waning or resurgence of the power they put into the fight more easily than I ever could with the long rods I once used.

Salmon rods are things to love and cherish. One tends to hang on to them for sentimental reasons and, therefore, the move to lighter rods has been slower than if they were items of short life, quickly discarded for a newer style. But when buying a new one it is wise to follow the general trend, which has been toward lighter tackle. Those who fish for trout as well as salmon may have a well-loved trout rod they can move up to their salmon fishing. The newer, lighter rods can then start to build up memories, locking them into the bamboo, glass or other fibers, to be cherished through times to come.

[1976]

CHAPTER FIFTEEN

How Fast the Fly?

Most veteran salmon fishermen will agree that in
wet-fly fishing, fly speed is the most important factor in moving
or failing to move a salmon. Many writers on salmon fishing have
made this point, but few have been able to explain accurately
just how fast the fly should be moving. Here's Wulff's answer to
that question, which should allow almost anyone to overcome
the initial hurdle of proper fly speed.

• • • • • • • • •

WHEN AN ANGLER presents a fly to a salmon, he has to consider
both the movement of the water relative to the fish and the
movement, if any, of the fly through (or over) the water. A dry

fly has no movement relative to the water in a free drift. A wet fly moving through still water has only the movement imparted by the angler. A sunken fly moving through flowing water takes on a combination of the speeds imparted by both angler and current.

Again, there are two basics to consider. The speed of the fly's *swim* through the water, and the pure speed of the fly in relation to the fish. The first is a matter of naturalness. How fast would an underwater insect swim, or an imitation insect move, in order to appear natural or attractive to a salmon? The second is a physical thing. How fast can or will a salmon move in order to catch a fly that goes flashing past him?

The speed of a fly's *swim* through the water is, in the minds of many, the key to success in conventional wet-fly fishing. It should be somewhere around two miles an hour. Each knowing angler will sense that speed as he watches his fly, just as a driver, accustomed to driving at fifty-five miles an hour, can judge that speed by watching the terrain go by instead of relying on his speedometer. As the current slows or increases in pace, the angler can raise his rod or take in line to increase his fly's speed relative to the water or he can lower his rod or let out line to slow his fly down. In this way, the angler will try to hold his fly at that perfect swim-speed with which he feels he has maximum success.

Years ago that perfect retrieve speed was very difficult to learn and achieve. The Portland Creek Hitch, which I brought to the attention of the salmon-angling fraternity in 1946, offers an easy way to see and learn to recognize that speed. The "hitching" of the fly calls for the wet fly to be tied on to the leader conventionally, then to have two half-hitches of the leader thrown around the fly just behind the tying thread of the head. With a single-hooked fly, the leader should come away from the fly at a forty-five-degree angle on the side of the fly so that it will skim the water with the bend of the hook downstream. This calls for the leader to come off on the left side if, as you face the stream to cast, the current is flowing to your left; off the right side if the current is flowing to the right. On a double-hooked fly, it should come away directly under the throat.

If the movement of the hitched fly is so swift that it tends to throw a little spray or bobble the surface, then the fly is moving too fast. If the speed is not great enough the fly will sink. The perfect speed lies somewhere in the range between bobbling and sinking. It's pretty much right at the midpoint between the two. By watching the fly's action, an angler can practice speeding up the fly and slowing it down as it passes through slower and swifter waters. When he has mastered the fly swim-speed with the hitched fly, he can transfer the same techniques to the invisible sunken fly and bring his capacity to draw wet- or skimming-fly rises to a maximum.

Normally, salmon lie in places where the swing of the current on a downstream cast angled across at about forty-five degrees will give a good presentation. As faster-than-normal flows are encountered, the downstream angle can be increased to, say, sixty degrees off the flow direction, and the fly slowed down by starting with a high rod and lowering it as the retrieve progresses. In slower water, the fly speed can be increased by a reverse maneuver. In dead-still water, both the rod lift and a pulling in of the line will be required.

A word of advice. Much as the perfect speed for the wet-fly retrieve should be the eternal goal, there will always be times when the rules should be broken. Sometimes, and especially in slow or still waters, the fastest possible retrieve will excite listless salmon and bring them to the fly. Conversely, the slowing of a fly to the best possible drift will bring rises where normal retrieves will not. This is the basis of the "greased line" or free-drift fly. Actually it is not a free drift. If it were, the fly could only go directly downstream as a free drifting dry fly does. With the "greased line" drift, the fly is cast at a normal wet-fly angle to the current and it ends up just where the conventional wet-fly cast would bring it. All the mending and rod movements have done is to keep the fly itself facing across the stream during as much of the cast as possible and, perhaps, slow its speed a little.

The dry-fly presentation is almost always with a completely free drift. But, even though it may seem to flash by the salmon lying in or under a swift run at too great a speed for them to catch it, that's rarely the case. I'm reminded of a pool on the Adlatok where the water raced over a lip at the tail and carried on down through fast broken water too rough to follow a salmon through. Ted Rogowski was flicking a dry fly out preparatory to casting up into the pool. His fly dropped to the swift tail race run and was whipped out of sight in a fraction of a second. But, in that brief instant, I thought I saw a flash of silver deep down under the water's race. At my suggestion, Ted dropped his fly in the race again, and again I saw a movement beneath it. The third cast brought a spray-throwing rise. The fish was hooked, but it was an exercise in futility. He turned down into the rocky chute and left a broken leader behind him. It was also a lesson in how swiftly a salmon can move. Many times since then I've fished dry flies in unbelievably fast water and hooked some salmon where they could be landed in spite of the fast water conditions at the point of the rise.

In conclusion, I will recommend seeking the perfect speed of retrieve for the wet fly and using the free drift of the dry fly for at least ninety percent of the time you fish.

Use the rest for experimenting. And I hope you'll try the very fast wet-fly retrieve and use a dry skater or put a few twitches to your dry fly before you give up on a particularly attractive piece of water.

[1976]

CHAPTER SIXTEEN

HOW AND WHEN TO CHANGE FLIES

*E*ven on those all-too-rare occasions when I've managed to put the right fly in the right place at the right time,
thereby catching a salmon, I'm left with a puzzle. In every case,
I know that the successful fly pattern doesn't work all the time,
and I'm left wondering what else might have worked to lure the
fish of the moment. I have sometimes taken salmon with fly
patterns far different from those used by other fishermen who
were equally successful on the same day and river. And I've more
often used more conventional flies to no avail. What I haven't
done is to change flies as thoughtfully as Wulff suggests in this
chapter, which may be the best answer of all.

Two of the most important questions facing the average salmon angler are how and when to change flies. Few of us are like the old-time salmon angler, one of the most successful I knew back in the thirties, who said, "It doesn't matter what kind of fly you use—jest as long as it's a Jock Scott."

The choice of flies was not so great back in those days when only the conventional and accepted salmon patterns were in use. Joe managed very well with just one fly. A. H. E. Wood of "greased line" fame, on the Aberdeenshire Dee, had narrowed his fly choices down to three: Blue Charm, Silver Blue and March Brown. Limited to those three flies he was a most successful salmon fisherman.

How much, one asks, is real and how much illusion when it comes to the effect of the change of fly on the fish? Is it the pause it takes to make the change, those minutes of rest, that makes the difference or is it really the difference between the old fly and the new? Suppose an angler fishes over a salmon steadily without changing his fly and on the 300th cast the salmon rises and is hooked. Suppose, again, that another angler changed his fly four times during an equal number of casts and then hooked his fish, too, on the 300th cast. Each could claim his method was the path to success and believe it—but neither could really prove it.

It's obvious that presentation is a major factor in success with the Atlantic salmon, but a great many anglers have proven that a great many *different* flies will take fish. It's hard to believe that any one fly or any dozen flies can completely cover the working spectrum of the salmon's susceptibility and give as fine a result as the perfect use of each of the many available patterns to match the particular circumstances prevailing.

It is true that most of us concentrate on a few flies in which we have great faith, but we all know that the time will come again and again when we fail to connect with our favorites and start reaching back into the crannies of our fly boxes for something strange or unusual. And we've found, to our pleasure, that these "strange" flies often work.

As a case in point, after fifteen days in Iceland I was feeling particularly smug because I'd never failed to catch at least one fish in each of the morning or afternoon fishing periods. It was our last afternoon, and there were fish all around us. Hours went by, and I couldn't draw a rise. In despair, having tried everything else, I put on a tandem fly that was of Jock Scott coloring and four inches long. On the fifth cast with that monstrosity I hooked a grilse, the only fish of the afternoon. (To my dismay, I lost him.)

It follows, therefore, that it is good to have anywhere from a dozen to several hundred "extra flies" in addition to those few in which we place great faith. It was worth carrying that strange fly around for five years just to have it when I needed something special.

When I started salmon fishing, the time-tested conventional patterns were the only ones being used. The silhouettes were much the same for all of them, and the size of the fly became the most important consideration. Basic shades and color tones were secondary. Most of the best fishermen felt that the dark fly, dark day/bright fly, bright day theory was a good one because a dark fly showed up best when seen from below against a low light in the sky. Many *anglers* would differ, though, on whether a Silver Gray or a Mar Lodge, which at first glance are twins, was better. I doubt if very many *salmon* would have differentiated between those two look-alikes, refusing to take one in favor of the other if the size of the flies were the same.

Presentation is paramount, I'll admit. Without good presentation there'll be little success. Assuming good presentation, how and when should one change the fly?

Starting out with wet flies there are two basic casts to use, and my first change, normally, is to go from a standard sunken fly cast to the riffling hitch or vice versa. Putting the two half hitches behind the head of the fly will make it skim the surface, and the difference between the skimming and the sunken fly is often enough to bring a reluctant fish from a sluggish rise to a real take. I make this change automatically if I raise a salmon that refuses to come back on the next cast or two. More often than not, the change will bring a reluctant riser to the steel.

Changing the fly pattern and size is, of course, a personal thing. When fishing is slow, my change is likely to be to a fly of a different category. Category changes are always more important, I believe, than simple pattern changes. To go from a standard #4 Jock Scott to a standard #4 Dusty Miller is a pattern change. To go from the Jock Scott to a Muddler Minnow of the same size is a change in category.

Some of the categories for wet flies are (1) standard, (2) hair fly, (3) low water, (4) muddler, (5) tube fly and (6) nymph (example: Woolly Worm). Each has a different *shape* and a different action in the water. I like to change categories, then sizes and, finally, patterns within the categories.

Dry flies came to salmon fishing not long before I did. In the beginning, dry-fly patterns were as routine as the wet-fly patterns of that day. Ed Hewitt brought the first big change with the Bivisible. Then he added the Spider or Skater, which had little effect at the time but is used to a greater and greater extent as a fly to fall back on. I made the next major one, I believe, when I put animal hair on dry flies to make them float higher and carry heavier bodies like the Gray, White and Royal Wulff flies. Preston Jennings developed a stonefly, and so did I. Both were in a new category. My Surface Stonefly has a long body and a hair wing lying down its back that makes it float low in the surface film. It takes a special cast to keep it up. Half wet, half dry, it can be drifted, then dragged. More than that, I know when I cast it out over hard-fished salmon that I'm shocking them a little with something they haven't seen before. Harry Darbee is reputed to have come up with the Rat-Faced McDougall, half dry fly and half bass bug, and created another new category and a new cult. I've added an offshoot on the Rat-Face, my "Advisory," which spreads whole looped hackles out on the surface film on each side of a long clipped deer-hair body, another of the floating-in-the-film flies but this time with a greater action and spread of wing.

These are the basics as things stand now, but dry-fly fishing for salmon, which is only half a century old, is due for continuing changes. New categories will be added. Our fishing will become more complete and, as it does, more effective for those with the knowledge and intuition as to when to use the new forms.

There are many minor variations that are serious enough to change the silhouette of a fly considerably without taking it completely out of a category. A palmer-tied dry fly, like the Pink Lady, for example, is half standard fly and half Bivisible. A fat-bodied, long-haired semiskater would fall halfway between a Rat-Face and a normal skater. The Prefontaine, another of my variations, is part skater and part Bivisible and set apart from the other dry flies by its forward-pointing, long bucktail snout to give it a rolling, tumbling action as it slides over the surface.

The method variations within the cast can be almost as important, sometimes, as a change of fly. If you know where a fish is, do you drop the wet fly just beyond him and swing it just over his nose time and time again or do you lengthen your line to make it approach him in a series of different approaches? When you put a dry fly over a good lie, do you drop it right where the fish lies or do you spot it well upstream and let it drift tantalizingly down to his resting place? Do you vary from one to the other, or do you make all your casts medium drifts that start your fly floating, let's say, seven or eight feet above the salmon's known lie?

The options are many, but I believe that the angler who has the widest capability of covering the widest number of categories in the right sizes, both wet and dry, and the judgment to use them well is the most deadly fisherman of all.

[1976]

CHAPTER SEVENTEEN

THE STRIKE

*T*here are many salmon-fishing trips whose duration is
measured by hours of fruitless casting, until the last day perhaps
when a reluctant salmon finally rises. The frustration that's been
building day after day often finds expression in the angler's strike
at that moment, which almost inevitably pulls the fly away from
the rising fish. There have been many times when I've wished I
had Wulff's salmon-fishing advice more firmly in mind, but none
more so than when I've failed to hook a salmon on the strike.

THE ANGLER HAS MADE cast after cast, living in the expectancy of
the strike. He waits. He hopes. He keeps casting. Suddenly the

strike comes. The angler's thoughts by this time may be far away. He sees the fish move toward his fly or, if he's looking away, he feels the pressure. He reacts.

If he sees the fish and it is coming to the fly in the tantalizingly deliberate way many salmon have of rising, the impatient or nervous angler often strikes at the "sight" and lifts the fly away before the salmon can reach it and close his mouth on it. Striking on sight and the empty feeling that follows is something almost every salmon angler has experienced.

Having it happen once should be enough for a lifetime, but I know a number of nervous anglers to whom it has happened many times because their reaction comes out of pure nervousness and is automatic rather than controlled. The wise and experienced angler will program his strike to the fly he has on and the leader he's using. When he changes the fly or the leader he reprograms his subconscious. This is not easy to accomplish, and no one I know does it perfectly. Those who come closest tend to "set" their usual strike as a light one and try to remember to strike hard when they put on a large hook. Underpowering is a bit safer than overpowering, where the result may well be a broken leader.

It is important to make sure that the hook is set. It is less obvious but probably more important to keep the strike below the power level that will break the leader or cut the flesh and start the hole that later playing will make large enough to let the hook fall free. A hard hook-setting involves a stronger pull over a longer period of time. That extra time may carry the pull into the beginning of the fish's reaction run and spell disaster.

The spread of power variation depends upon the spread of the hook sizes and rods the angler uses. If he always fishes with strong leaders, all his strikes may well be as strong as his tackle will stand. If he ranges down under ten pounds for leaders and into the small fly range, he'll have to vary his strikes accordingly.

If the fish is docile, strikes on the hard side won't cause too many problems, but if the fish's reaction is as swift as the strike, and just as hard, even the strongest leaders will break and hooks will tear right through a grip that would hold under ordinary circumstances.

The strike with a conventional wet fly and the strike for a normal, free-floating dry fly are completely different. The wet fly moves through the water and its very movement will bring it in contact with the fish's jaws. The dry fly floats freely, giving the salmon slack enough to spit it out unless the angler sets the hook. The salmon angler must vary his strike to suit the situation.

Many anglers feel the need to strike no matter what the fly or the method. Others are confident the salmon will hook himself on a wet fly. Must one strike with a wet fly? The answer is yes and no. Yes, when the wet fly is moving slowly or is on a large, dull or double-pronged hook. No, when the fly is moving swiftly or the hook is small or sharp and requires little pull to penetrate beyond the barb.

How do you program yourself to strike when necessary and to strike with suitable vigor or restraint as the occasion demands? The need is to set the hook beyond the barb so it cannot draw back. The main variable is the size of the hook, the key to the power required to *set* each particular fly. A second factor is the strength of the leader, which enters into the picture only when it is relatively light. Obviously the strike required to set a small hook like a #12 is a gentle one; the strike need for a 3/0 double hook must be fierce. Whether the hook is large or small, the force required to set a double hook is more than twice that needed for a single of the same size.

Balancing the leader to the hook size is wise, if not essential. If the change is made from a small fly to a larger one or to a double hook, the leader that was balanced for the first may break or the hook fail to penetrate. The single-hook angler in the smaller hook sizes of from 12 to 6 has an advantage. His hooks will set quickly and surely on a light strike. A light strike, where the fish misses the fly, may not frighten him, and he'll come back again on a later cast. If the strike is a vicious one, he'll pull off completely.

So the angler will watch his wet fly—or watch the water where he thinks the fly is swimming. He will try to match the salmon's deliberation with a restraint and deliberation of his own. He will not initiate his striking pull until he is sure the salmon has the fly in his mouth.

The way to be sure the salmon has taken the fly is to wait till the salmon closes his mouth and the fly, in contact with his mouth, pulls on the line. At that precise instant the angler should set the hook.

Tradition says that at the instant of the strike the angler should raise his rod and shout exultantly, whether there is anyone around to hear him or not, "I've got one on!" Then tradition would have him lean back and enjoy the beautiful fierce bend of his rod and (if he hasn't struck hard enough to break the fish off) the song of the reel as the fish races away. Let me caution you not to follow this tradition.

Many years ago when I began trying to get good pictures, both still and moving, I took a cameraman with me when I fished. Being a cameraman with an angler can be a difficult and challenging job. It can also be boring as the devil. There you stand, at alert, with your camera at the ready, and this fellow fishing has already cast a million times and hooked nothing. You may begin wondering how he can stand the monotony of the incessant, fruitless casting without any result. It's now 3:00 and this nut has been casting steadily since 7:30 A.M. You're thirsty.

So you go over to the canoe, put your camera on the seat and pick up a bottle of Coke. You've just popped the cap and the bottle is halfway to your lips when this fisherman shouts out, "I've got one on!"

You drop your Coke to the sand and grab your camera. A cloud has passed over the sun and you check the shutter speed and distance setting and point your camera out at the pool in general as you hear your angler shouting, "Did you get those jumps?"

You say, "What jumps?" and he calls on the Lord to smite you down. " 'What jumps?' Those were the best jumps a salmon ever made. Where the hell were you?"

For the fisherman it brings the realization that the cameraman has missed the best jumps *again*. It makes you think. You study the problem. How can I, the fisherman, control this fish? How can I let him or make him jump only when I want him to? And I came up with a solution.

This fish jumps in reaction to the sudden pressure I put on him. If I don't put any pressure on him, will he jump? What will he do? If he just has a fly prick in his jaw and nothing more, why shouldn't he go right back to his lie? After all that's where he chose to be and I think that's where he'll go. Perhaps he'll shake his head or work his jaws to see if he can spit the fly out or shake it free, but—probably—nothing more.

If the hook is into his jaw beyond the barb, it won't fall out no matter how slack the line. He'll just wait there until my cameraman is ready and I've told him exactly where to point the camera. Then I'll put on the pressure, and he'll jump for a beautiful picture.

That's how it worked when I tried it, long, long ago. Net result: the cameraman could be relaxed instead of under constant tension keeping the camera pointed at my fly. I got the jumps I wanted by putting pressure on again when I wanted him to jump. And I learned a lot more about playing fish through making movies.

So your object with the strike should be to set the hook, nothing more.

The question often comes up, "If the angler waits for a pull on the line before he strikes, can the salmon that has taken his wet fly spit it out without getting hooked?"

He can, perhaps, but he'd have to be so fast I'd be very surprised if he could make it—and so suspicious that I doubt if he'd have taken that fly in the first place. If it happens, it will be because the angler was using a double-hooked fly and the fish, in closing his mouth, felt the hard, sharp pressure of the double steel. A single hook, lying flat in a salmon's mouth, is much harder for him to detect as a fraud, and the full closing of the mouth will take more time. Or it will be because the angler did not react to the pressure of the fish and the fly was moving so slowly that the hook did not embed and the fish could spit it out.

It matters little whether the wet fly is fished conventionally sunken or surface skimmed with a "riffling" hitch. The movement of the fly relative to the water is the same as is the tension of the fly on the line. The main difference is that in order to take the hitched fly the salmon will have to show himself at the surface. This means that the angler is more likely to see the salmon *before* he takes the fly and to strike early, while with the sunken fly, unless the fish makes a head and tail rise, the first indication the fisherman will have that there's a salmon near his fly is the pull on the line.

There is no way in the world to make every strike perfect. I can recall losing one big salmon at the strike that I had worked over long and hard for several evenings. He was a big hook-billed male in the thirty-pound range. When he finally came to the fly I lifted my rod in what I believed to be an ample strike for the #8 double I'd finally put on when all my single-hook choices had failed. The rod came tight, and I felt the fish solidly on the line.

I wanted him to drop back to his lie and rest there while I got the casting slack back onto the reel so I could play him directly from the reel when he felt pressure and ran out into the deeper water.

Before the slack line was half reeled in under pressure so light it wouldn't disturb him, I lost the feeling of even that slight pressure and he was gone.

In thinking long and hard about it later, I decided that both of the sharp hook points had struck a bony part of his mouth and that they hadn't penetrated, even though the strike would have been adequate under normal circumstances. I had the fly on a six-pound tippet since the water was low and he was wary. Had I been using an eight-pound tippet, and therefore struck a little harder, one of the barbs might have been set. I feel sure that if I had struck much harder than I did, I would have parted the leader and failed to catch him anyway.

A special strike, which at the time was quite revolutionary, was that developed by Arthur H. E. Wood for his greased-line type of fishing on the Aberdeenshire Dee in Scotland. He stressed, in his method, the free drift of a single-hooked wet fly kept near but just under the surface by greasing and floating his line and his leader to within an inch or two of the fly.

His technique was developed back in the twenties and was in reality the making of no strike at all. Because the drift of his fly was leisurely, he counted on a leisurely rise from the salmon. He was right, and the most frequent rise to the drifting fly was a slow head-and-tail take. Wood used small, low-water flies and as the fish returned to his lie near the bottom, the current's pull drew the fly into the corner of the mouth where the flesh is soft and hooking most certain. The pressure of his first movement would embed the hook. He felt that if an angler using his method failed to hook his fish in the corner of the mouth, he had not been fishing it properly. His system of striking worked very well and proved the point that a slow and deliberate tightening of the line is a very good hook-setting technique for wet-fly fishing.

The greased-line system does not give a truly free-drifting fly. The cast is made much like a conventional wet-fly cast, but the angle is a little more across the stream. The fly moves with the current just as the wet fly does and ends up in the same position a wet fly would on the same cast. It ends up well downstream of the caster. The only difference is that the line is "mended" during the drift to keep the fly itself perpendicular to the flow. Other than that, greased-line fishing parallels fishing the wet. Consequently, the greased-line wet fly is actually moving through the water constantly and, like a wet fly, which is tight on the line all the time, will tend to hook fish without a strike.

The dry fly, on the contrary, is normally fished with a completely free drift with bends and coils for slack in the leader and line. It calls for a different kind of a strike. Except for unusual cases, where there is little slack and the water is moving along well so that the line tightens swiftly and the fish will hook himself, the dry-fly fisherman must either take the slack out of the line and add a hook-setting pressure with his rod or he must strike

through the slack to move the hook enough to embed it. The first
type is a *rod* strike and the second a *line* strike. When a dry-fly
fisherman must overcome a *lot* of slack, he will want to combine
both types to be sure he gets enough pressure. The rod strike
is the typical wet-fly strike. The line strike is a supplemental strike
that can be used with a free-drifting dry fly.

Consider a rope thrown out on the ground. It has fallen
loosely, and there are waves and slack places in it. Pick up one
end of the rope and give it a hard, swift yank. The movement
is not enough to straighten out the rope completely—far from
it. But it will send an impulse the entire length and move the
far end a few inches in the direction of the yank. The movement
necessary to set a #6 hook is less than three-sixteenths of an
inch. Such a movement can be generated in a fly by a sharp pull
of the line in the left hand *even if the rod is held steady.* The
combination of a line pull and a rod lift makes the setting of the
dry-fly hook most certain.

The short, sharp movement of the left hand is swift, and its
energy, too, is swiftly spent. On such a strike the hook is set, and
then slack is given again. The lift of the rod takes more power
and that power must be controlled. Too hard a rod strike will
break a leader if, while the power is being applied to the rod,
the salmon decides to add the power of his own movement of
the fly in the opposite direction. It takes only a millisecond of
overpowering to snap a leader.

How much slack can an angler have around his free-floating
dry fly and still be able to set the hook? An awful lot. Even with
very short rods I feel competent to set the hook no matter how
much slack I throw into the cast.

These are the mechanics of the dry-fly strike. Remember that
dry-fly hooks are single, fine wire and sharp. They set easily.
Strike only when the fly goes out of sight in the salmon's mouth.
Watch the fly. A salmon may come up, open his mouth and close
it again without taking the fly. He may poke the fly up into the
air on his nose with his mouth closed. The dry-fly fisherman
must watch his fly and should never strike till he's sure. If it's

the missed rise of a play maneuver by the fish and the fly goes merrily on, the salmon may come back again. If the fly is snatched brusquely out from under his nose on a false rise, he'll probably be offended and sulkily refuse any further flies.

With a free-drifting wet fly or nymph there is never the great amount of slack to be found in dry-fly fishing. If the cast is made and a nymph or wet fly drifts along freely, it sings as it goes and maintains a tension, though a very slight one, on the fly at all times. The fish, taking this free-drifting sunken fly and moving away with it, pulls against the drag on the line *even if there is not strike*. That tends to embed the hook point. Then either a swift movement of the fish or a lift of the rod by the angler will set the hook.

There are two other categories to consider. First, there is the dry fly that is dragged across the surface on a typical wet-fly cast (with a greased line and leader). That calls for the same strike a wet fly does. Second, there is the skater or twitched dry fly that skids on the surface in a jerky retrieve. As with all the surface-riding flies, the angler usually sees the fish before he closes his mouth on the fly. The worry is striking too soon and too hard. Success lies in good timing and just the right amount of power.

[1977]

CHAPTER EIGHTEEN

THE COHO PROBLEM

*F*ortunately for the Atlantic salmon, management atti-
tudes are slowly changing to favor indigenous fish species rather
than the sometimes helter-skelter introductions and stockings of
nonnative fish of years past. New Hampshire's experiments with
coho-salmon stocking in the Northeast, as described in this 1977
chapter, haven't been particularly successful. As fishery agencies
all over the country now face times of reduced and uncertain
budgets, one may hope that such environmental vandalism will
diminish further as it typically offers a lower return for tax dollars spent than money spent for the enhancement of more de-
sirable native species.

IF YOU WANDER through the halls of the American Museum of Natural History in New York where the skeletons of long-extinct animals stand stark and bare as ghostly reminders of long ago and you look up to a certain wall, you'll see a plaque. It reads, "The presence in one community of two or more kinds of animals with ways of life similar in some essential respect is always temporary. If the immigrants are successful enough they tend to replace their native competitors."

Coho (*Oncorhynchus kisutch*) is one of the varieties of Pacific salmon. It is a good gamefish, but where West Coast anglers have a choice, the preference is consistently for rainbow or steelhead trout. The coho is primarily a saltwater gamefish, caught mainly in the estuaries where it is at the peak of its health. As soon as it enters the river on its spawning run, it starts to deteriorate chemically in a process that causes its death after spawning. As a gamefish the Atlantic salmon *Salmo salar* far outshines it.

The coho is, however, a better commercial fish than the Atlantic salmon because the coho parr usually stay in the rivers less than a year before going to sea, while the Atlantics stay several years, on the average. Thus, the food supply of a given river will produce several times as many coho parr to go to sea and come back weighing many more pounds of "salmon" for a commercial fishery. It is the commercial interests that are behind the introduction of coho and other Pacific salmon species in present or potential Atlantic salmon waters.

In Newfoundland between 1959 and 1966 about 15 million pink salmon (a Pacific type) eggs were planted in the hope of developing commercial fishery. The stock failed to sustain itself, and the attempt was considered a failure for that species at that time and place. Of all the Pacific species tried in the Atlantic, the coho has been the most successful.

In New England the United States National Marine Fisheries Service, whose interest has traditionally been overwhelmingly commercial, when faced with a choice of spending its funds on restoring Atlantic salmon to its original habitat where it was once plentiful and valuable for both commercial and sport fisheries or bringing in the exotic coho, chose the coho with a statement that this was something special for the sportsman.

Their selected site was New Hampshire, a state with eighteen miles of coastline and no major river mouth but which also has hundreds of miles of upstream waters where Atlantic salmon once thrived and, we hope, will thrive again. The New Hampshire Fish and Game Commission has for over two years consistently voted to eliminate this coho program, which, they feel, is not a wise expenditure of the sportsmen's license monies. Pressure from commercial interests on the New Hampshire legislature has kept it alive. This year, the commission again has eliminated the coho program from its budget. The New Hampshire legislature will decide before July whether or not to override the commission's decision.

Coho proponents say it is a stopgap, and that when Atlantic salmon are restored to New England they can then eliminate the coho that are being maintained by hatchery stockings, but that in the interim they will provide some sport that would not otherwise be available. The great coho fishery that developed after their introduction into Lake Michigan called for special boats and equipment. It seems highly unlikely that once the local anglers have bought the special boats and equipment any government could get away with saying "Now it's time to scrap your investment and buy fly rods. We won't give you any more cohos."

The coho-fishing success in Lake Michigan came about because commercial overfishing and attacks by lamprey eels had all but eliminated the predator fish of the lake. When alewives, a forage fish, were introduced they got out of hand and multiplied so rapidly that there were thousands of tons of dead alewives drifting onto the beaches near Chicago to perfume the air and spoil the areas for swimming and recreation. The introduction of a predator fish was in order, and the coho was chosen over rainbow trout that would have done the job just as well.

The coho did its job and thrived beyond wildest expectations. A new fishery was born that made a lot of anglers happy with the trolling it offered in the "substitute sea" of Lake Michigan, but it upset more people than it pleased with the "snagging frenzy" it brought to the trout rivers flowing into the lake.

Any type of salmon may stray, and the farther they are stocked from their point of origin the more likely straying is to occur. Coho and Atlantic salmon in the same river will obviously compete for spawning grounds. The parr of the coho, which grow much more rapidly, will compete with Atlantic salmon parr for food in the rivers, and the coho parr can actually grow fast enough to eat young Atlantic salmon spawned at the same time. It is reasonable to assume that, having similar capabilities and needs, these coho will also seek out and utilize competitively the same great food sources of the northern seas upon which the Atlantic salmon have historically fed. The coho seems to be a better competitor and the one destined to survive if its proponents manage to set up a duel to the death.

Now there is an attempt to introduce coho salmon to Scotland for commercial fish farming. It is meeting stiff resistance from Atlantic salmon anglers. But if this effort fails there will be another attempt and another, wherever rivers of the Atlantic are suitable for salmon. The underlying reasons will always be the Pacific salmon's greater value in commerce and the claim that they give a "soon-to-start-starving" world a greater supply of protein from the sea. The question becomes whether or not man lives "by bread alone" and whether those who believe that life should mean more than just staying alive can or will muster the forces necessary to preserve the magnificent Atlantic salmon and a sport they love and believe in.

[1977]

CHAPTER NINETEEN

BRING THE BOYS

I *have found in taking my own children fishing that the better part of wisdom is usually silence. This isn't easy. But I know that when I spout a fountain of instructions, all intended to help them catch fish, that I instead diminish the value of their fishing experience by confusing them with more than they can handle at one time. Better to let them fish and make their own mistakes. They'll learn more that way, I've found, and are better able to enjoy their fishing, which is what I hope for in the first place. Wulff struggles heroically with that problem in this chapter, showing a remarkable patience with his novice salmon anglers.*

THE INVITATION SAID "Bring the boys, if you wish. You can have the camp for three days." That meant a chance to take Stuart and Michael to the Big Salmon River in New Brunswick to fish for Atlantic salmon.

We thought about it a lot. Would these teenagers really appreciate the opportunity? Would their concentration span be too short to cope with the sophisticated salmon? Would we be giving them something too complicated for them to enjoy?

Another factor entering into the picture was the future of salmon fishing itself. I have more than a faint fear that the opportunity to fish for this great fly-rod species is dwindling to a point where it will become too difficult for the average American to find or afford. And I know that no one in the future will have an opportunity to cover the wild and productive waters as I once did or to catch as many fish. In a sense, I think, we were hoping to pass on to the boys some of the experience we'd gained so that they might understand and enjoy whatever salmon opportunities they'd have to the fullest.

When the letter came my thoughts had flashed back to my own first trip for Atlantic salmon. I had really graduated to it. I was twenty-eight and had put many years on the trout streams. I had read the books and dreamed my dreams and saved until I could afford a trip to Nova Scotia.

When my first salmon, a ten-pounder, rose to the #8 Grizzly Bivisible in the Hut Pool on the Margaree I was so excited I can still remember seeing the little black spots on his gill covers as he came up through the crystal-clear water to take the fly. I measured the length of his body in my mind. Setting the hook was instinctive. When the great silvery fish made his first leap and run and my rod bent into a vibrating arc, it was a dramatic moment. I was hooked for life. No other fish has offered me the same challenge. Atlantic salmon fishing has been, throughout a fishing lifetime, the stuff of dreams.

My wife, Joan, has a similar feeling for these fish. She had fished for trout and tarpon and a host of other fish before I introduced her to the Atlantic salmon, and they brought her, too, a brilliance of sport she treasures.

How much would the boys appreciate it? We'd have to wait and see.

Stuart Cummings, Joan's son, was just fifteen. Michael Salvato, her nephew, was sixteen. Both had caught some trout and other fish on a fly, but neither was really adept with a fly rod. In Michael's case this trip meant leaving preseason football practice, taking a lot of ragging about lack of school spirit and being called, derisively, "the fisherman." But he came freely, as Stuart did, with a happy heart.

We had been told that the salmon of the Big Salmon River enter the river in late August and that our time, August 29 to September 1, would be one of the best. Our arrival at the stream gave us a rude shock: The salmon had entered the river in early July and had been in the camp's warm low-water pools for almost two months, during which time they'd been hard fished practically every day. If one wanted tough conditions with which to initiate someone to Atlantic salmon fishing it would be difficult to find anything tougher.

"The fish are there, all right,"said Greg Martin, the camp's head guide. "But they're hard to bring to a fly. A change of weather or a rise of water would help, but right now there's no rain in prospect."

I knew the conditions. I'd seen dead, low water many times before and usually, by fluke or intuition, had been successful in catching a fish or two. Now we wanted the kids to catch the fish. Could they manage it? I put aside my doubts, knowing they'd give it a good try.

Our first fishing in the Big Salmon came in the early light of a foggy dawn. We walked onto a platform that had been built out from a steep bank to overhang the pool. The water was clear and the stones of the streambed were relatively light in color. We could see a dozen salmon, motionless shapes that we mentally translated into pounds of angling treasure. The pounds, we calculated, ranged from six up to more than twenty. Greg pointed to them with pride. Then he helped Mike and Stuart check their tackle and gave each one of them a fly he'd tied. Both were variations of the Bomber, a clipped deer-hair sausage on a long-shanked #4 hook with a palmer wind of red or yellow hackle.

While the boys were working to tie on their flies there was a great splash out in the pool. We looked up to see the tail of a salmon disappearing beneath the surface. Before that splash had subsided the same salmon or another like him hurtled into the air and fell back in a twisting leap. The flies were tied on in a hurry.

First Mike and then Stuart dropped flies to the surface and let them float over the salmon spread out in the four-foot-deep flow. They fished with a quiet intensity. There was no sound except the low rustle of the river and the whisper of the fly lines in the air. They cast intently—but fruitlessly. They changed flies and alternated in their casting, but I could see no interest shown by any salmon.

The sun sent shining fingers of light over the mountains that hemmed us in, dissipating the fog—another hot, dry day to come. I heard remarks such as, "I think he moved that time" or "Didn't that one turn to look at it?" From where I watched I couldn't see that a single salmon had moved a muscle.

The hours crawled by and the boys, as we had anticipated, began to lose enthusiasm. Finally the effects of the previous day's travel and the early hour of rising took their toll. The boys stretched out like rag dolls on the bare rocks of the dry streambed, still clutching their rods.

At ten Greg piloted us up the quarter-mile path to the lodge's second pool, the Miller. From the shore he pointed out the areas in which the salmon should be lying and, taking Stuart in tow, started him casting into the swift run at the head of the pool. Joan and I sat on the bank to watch Michael fish the lower half.

The boys still needed tutoring in casting but were able to get their flies out forty or forty-five feet. I watched Michael's #6 White Wulff land and bounce beside a rock sunk in the flow. It drifted a foot or two and then there was a splash as a salmon sucked it down. Michael stood transfixed, making no move to strike. The fly appeared again as a white blob on the surface. With his eyes staring at the spot, Michael whispered a fervent "Holy smoke!" Then the pool was quiet again.

I could see grim determination on his face as he turned back to the river and cast the white fly out to drift in the slow current again. I wandered up over the dry rocks to watch Stuart casting a wet fly under Greg's careful coaching.

When the boys finally tired of fruitless casting we three tried our luck. Greg, in particular, felt he was going to catch a fish since he had the most knowledge about the river. He had been its warden for years before becoming camp manager and head guide. Like the boys, we were blanked completely. At noon we headed in for lunch.

There are two sets of conditions under which a salmon river becomes almost useless to fish. We were experiencing one. The other comes when there is a very heavy rain. As the water begins to rise, when the river has come up two or three inches, there'll be a period of fly-taking interest by the fish. But as the river continues to rise they'll stop taking flies and no one will catch a fish until after the flood has crested and the river steadies or starts to fall. This may take several days.

Our weather held hot and dry, and the fish remained indifferent. We fished the mornings and again in the late evenings. In the afternoons we gave the fish a rest. The boys got casting lessons then. They could cast fairly well but lacked little touches, such as fully straightening out wet-fly casts and putting the right amount of slack in casts with the dry.

During the first evening we concentrated on the Miller Pool with its shallower water and more rocky flow. There's a general feeling that salmon take a fly better if the water is shallow and moving well. This time Michael went to the head of the pool with Greg while Stuart waded out to fish the long, slow flow at the tail.

Later that evening I explained that the best way to fish for leaping salmon is mentally to mark the spot where a fish leaps and don't cast there immediately. Instead, wait till the fish has a chance to build up restlessness again because it probably leaped to relieve tension. It's the restless fish that takes a fly. There's an old saying that leaping fish won't take a fly, and I think it came from anglers who fished them immediately after they made a leap. I've caught salmon I saw leap, after giving them time to build up tension again, and then found by careful survey they were the only salmon in the pool at the time.

There were so many things I wanted to tell Stuart, but it would take time. There on the pool I said nothing. I just let him feel the excitement of having these great fish leap around him and of casting to each one as it leaped while the memory burned bright in his mind.

I watched his fly as intently as he did so I saw a salmon roll up beneath it, breaking the surface but just playing with, not actually taking, the fly. Stuart struck quickly and when he failed to hook the fish he turned to give me a rueful look.

I just said, "Try him again. He may come back," even though I knew the odds were against it.

Later I would tell him that Atlantic salmon often *play* with a dry fly, particularly under low-water conditions. They'll just pole at it with their mouths closed or they'll try to drown it under their chins or sink it with a swish of their tails. A wise and experienced angler will be watching his dry fly so closely that if he sees the salmon hasn't taken the fly into its mouth he'll let it drift right on. When a salmon makes a false rise and the fly is snatched away, he'll be, as we say, "insulted," and there's little chance he'll come back.

For two more days and a final morning we worked those salmon over. Once I saw Michael's rod bend down sharply on a wet-fly cast and when I saw Greg take off his fly-laden hat and crush it between his hands in dismay, I knew Mike had come awfully close to hooking a good fish.

The most dramatic moment was Stuart's on the final morning. His dry fly had drifted in close, and he started to pick it up for a new cast when a salmon shot up from below to take it. He struck with vigor, but the salmon was coming toward him and the line stayed slack, failing to set the hook. The salmon's rush carried it into the air right in front of the boy and hardly had the splash of the first leap flattened before it leaped again, even closer, to land almost at his feet. Then the fish vanished with a swirl of its tail and Stuart's line still hung slack. His eyes were as big as saucers.

Next day, when we were driving back, a few scattered drops of rain hit the windshield. I thought of the salmon. In the deluge that followed I could picture those fish in "our" pools. I could imagine the excitement that surged through them as the rain freshened the water. They would know that the river would rise and the water cool off soothingly. The spawning ground would beckon. But before they left the pool they would take the flies of lucky anglers who followed us and give *them* the excitement of playing great silvery fish.

I was sad that we would not have the chance those fishermen would have. Yet, I was glad that we had come and that the boys had seen the bitter side of salmon fishing and, I thought, accepted it. Greg Martin had been particularly good for them with his special knowledge of the fish and his tales of the river. Now they knew, as all dedicated salmon anglers eventually learn, how trying salmon fishing can be. Still, under those difficult conditions they had *almost* caught one.

They were already talking about "next year" and discussing fly patterns they had learned to tie in the evenings at camp. They were hooked on Atlantic salmon and blessed with a deeper understanding of the fish than most anglers acquire so swiftly. They knew that no salmon ever *has* to take a fly. But that even under the worst conditions there's always a chance. For them, forevermore, the Atlantic salmon will be a very special fish.

I know they'll never see the kind of fishing I had back in the thirties. I know, too, that as the fishing pressure increases, the opportunities in Canada and Europe will dwindle, year by year. The one bright spot is that they may not have to travel to foreign soil for fine salmon fishing.

There were more salmon caught in the Bangor Pool on Maine's Penobscot River last year than at any time since 1882. This year, for the first time in a century, a male and female salmon that had returned to a spawning run up the Connecticut River were mated. They produced more than 8,000 fertilized eggs that are now in a hatchery, growing toward the stage where they can be put in the Connecticut River system to help us build a native strain again.

One day, perhaps not more than a dozen years from now, Stuart and Michael may fish for Atlantic salmon in a tributary of the Connecticut that flows near our home. I may not live to see the great silvery runs returning in something like their old-time abundance, but I hope Stuart and Michael will. Then, because they will have come to understand these intriguing, exciting fish, they'll not only enjoy fishing for them but will cherish and help protect them for future generations to enjoy.

[1978]

CHAPTER TWENTY

SANCTUARY FOR THE SALMON

*F*ishing for Atlantic salmon—both commercially and for sport—is regulated by politicians wherever salmon are found. As such, it's ultimately regulated by votes. The greater the number of fishermen concerned with the salmon's future, the more powerful their ballot-box voice becomes—something of which Wulff was keenly conscious. His suggestion in this 1978 chapter on spinning tackle and salmon fishing will strike many as being wildly radical, but for the salmon's benefit those suggestions may be a wise choice.

I'VE OFTEN WISHED that spinning had been invented earlier. I wish that that devastating method had been in when the "surface fly fishing only" regulations on this continent were first set up. Then, I believe, the regulations would have said, simply, "Single-hook surface artificial lure fishing only" for Atlantic salmon.

Then spin fishermen would not feel discriminated against as they do now, and they would not have been any more than the fly fisherman who wants to use weight and fish deep is now discriminated against.

The salmon need a sanctuary to survive. That sanctuary is the deeper water in which they lie. As long as the angler must fish a lure in such a manner as to cause the salmon to leave his lie and come to, or near, the surface to take it, the fishing will be most sporting and the numbers of salmon taken will stay, I believe, within reasonable limits. The object of the regulations would be to keep flies and lures out of the depths the salmon lie in.

Whether a lure is cast with a fly rod, as a fly cast behind a floating bubble with a spinning rod or as a surface popper cast by a baitcasting outfit, in every case the salmon should have to be *lured out of his position* of rest to make a serious movement toward the surface to be hooked and captured.

Although the regulation of "surface fly fishing only" is now well established and would be difficult to change, the advantages of such an action may outweigh the difficulties.

If "surface fishing only" were permitted it would allow for the use of specified lures that would not go more than a few inches under the surface on the retrieve. It would take away the feeling that Atlantic salmon fishing is being withheld from the public at large by *method* and saved for the elite, which means that when the population's votes are cast the "masses" may have many and that the "elite" have few to change the method.

I think it is unfortunate, too, that double-hooked flies, heavy enough to sink readily to the bottom, have been permitted for Atlantic salmon fishing. The "patent" method of fly fishing calls for trying to put such a fly into the salmon's mouth as he rests near the bottom. Then, when the angler feels a fish take the fly, he yanks to set the hook. If he simply yanks when the fly sinks to the area in which the salmon is lying he'll often foul-hook the fish. In fact, the angler who wants to foul-hook a salmon simply fishes the patent cast. A little lead will make the fly sink faster and is used when the current is swift or the "jigger" not skillful enough to judge the upstream distance necessary for a heavy double-hook fly to sink adequately. The fly is cast upstream to a point from which on a free drift, at its normal sink rate, it will drift right to the salmon. I have watched salmon under those circumstances open their mouths to take a passing fly and, because the angler was not quick to strike, spit it out again. I have seen fish foul-hooked with unweighted double-hook flies by fishermen who were good at the sink-on-the-drift technique. The outlawing of double hooks (which make foul-hooking easy while single hooks make it difficult) would save a lot of salmon. It would save more salmon, I believe, than would be lost if salmon fishing were opened to surface fishing only with single-hooked artificial lures with any type tackle. Opening Atlantic salmon fishing to a wider range of tackle may be the best political move possible under our present situation of pressure from non-fly-fishing groups.

While I am personally devoted to the fly rod for salmon, I believe an opportunity to use other types of tackle within a sporting restriction of this type could be a worthwhile move. The salmon in our rivers need a deep-water sanctuary just as much as our citizens need their homes as their inviolate castles. If we can give it to them, and at the same time gain more friends for them, the salmon conservation situation will have been improved. It has been said that in the political field "an unknown river has no friends." The more friends and admirers the Atlantic salmon has in political places in these times of change, the better its chances. It is something to think about.

[1978]

CHAPTER TWENTY-ONE

SALMON DIFFER

*B*ecause Atlantic salmon return unerringly to their natal river for spawning, these same salmon are genetically isolated from other populations of the same species in other rivers. As such they are subject to subtle adaptive and evolutionary pressures that vary from river to river. Wulff provides several examples of that kind of variation in this chapter, which also underscore a point that he makes elsewhere in this book: that salmon management is best undertaken on a river-by-river basis, an approach that best accounts for the differences among salmon strains.

IT IS NOW GENERALLY ACCEPTED that the salmon of each river—and often each major branch of the larger rivers—are a different strain. Long ago we knew that salmon varied with the rivers. The salmon that came into the two major rivers of Hawke Bay, Newfoundland, the East and the Torrent, were very different in shape. So were the salmon that came into Sandwich Bay in Labrador via the North River and the Eagle.

It was easy to see why they were different because the East River and the North River were long, rough rivers and hard for the salmon to travel while the flows of the Eagle and the Torrent were comparatively easy. The North and East rivers had long and slender salmon; the Eagle had typically shaped ones; the Torrent, which has a short and easy flow below the high falls blocking salmon from the upper river, had stocky fish, short and heavy, like those of two other rivers with slow and easy flows, the lower Humber and the Moisie.

The salmon of the East River and the North River were relatively easy to catch. Those of the Eagle seemed normal and those of the Torrent rather reluctant to take the fly. Catching a salmon at the mouth of a river you've never traveled can tell you a good deal about the character of the river. Conversely, flying over a river from source to mouth can tell you a lot about the character of the salmon that run it. How much it tells about the fly-taking habits of the fish is uncertain, but I am sure these habits vary just as much as the physical appearance does. I believe the slimmer fish will take larger flies, on the average, and take them more readily than the chunkier fish of the deep, slow rivers.

These differences are relative to certain areas, those of small watersheds. What about on a larger scale? I have found a basic difference between the salmon of this continent and those of Europe. The European salmon do not jump as freely when hooked. I can remember well a hook-jawed male salmon of more than twenty-five pounds from Newfoundland's Serpentine River that made twenty-two magnificent jumps before he gave in. Many of this continent's salmon have jumped a dozen times for me, but no European salmon has come close to that number. It has been my experience that a Canadian fish will jump twice as often, on the average, as one from Scotland or Norway. My experience on the Icelandic rivers indicates that those salmon fall about halfway between the two.

Another basic difference is in their willingness to take the dry fly. In Iceland, this difference can be due perhaps to the lack of hatches, and to the fact that the Icelandic salmon are not conditioned as parr to take insects from the surface. But such is not the case with Scottish rivers where there is a good deal of insect life and good hatches in the spring. To the surprise of many, I took a salmon on a dry fly in the Dee in 1962 although George LaBranche, fishing years earlier, had given it a good try and failed. It is easier to catch a salmon on a dry fly, I believe, in almost any salmon river in our native streams than in Europe and Iceland.

These variations in salmon character and behavior are things an angler should always keep in mind. If the salmon are not conditioned to a given behavior, then neither should we, as anglers, be stereotyped in our angling. It is one of the fascinating facets of salmon fishing that each river, each fish, each day and each hour may offer the angler a slightly different problem. The Jock Scott, on a conventional cast, will take salmon in any river but ingenuity and judgment in the use of flies of many types and patterns will not only make the sport more interesting but bring many more salmon to the steel.

[1979]

CHAPTER TWENTY-TWO

SEX IN SALMON-FLY SELECTION

On a recent fall trip to the headwaters of Labrador's *Eagle River, I encountered for the first time what must have been sex-related salmon fishing. No, it wasn't especially lurid, just unusual. Over the last three weeks of the season, some thirty salmon had been taken by camp guests, and all of those salmon were males. I added five more males to this total and didn't see a female fish all week.*

Since salmon runs are a typical mix of males and females, I have to assume that only the males were responding to our flies. At that late point in the season, the salmon had been in the river for a long time and had darkened to the point of resembling large brown trout (to which they're closely related). It appeared that the salmon were close to spawning, and the males may have been striking from some territorial or aggressive sense while the preoccupied female fish ignored our best angling efforts.

·········

PETER MCELLIGOTT, friend and fine salmon fisherman, says he fishes differently for male and female salmon. He fishes the Margaree late in the season, therefore his may be a special case. With spawning just around the corner, Peter feels that the males become territorial and are resentful of anything that comes within their chosen domains. As a result, for the males he uses fair-size or large flies and moves them swiftly through the area he believes a male has staked out.

It takes a good eye to tell a male from a female salmon, particularly in the early season. Distinguishing the slightly larger head size or heavier lower jaw as a fish lies in a pool, or even when he jumps, is something that few can bet on. Later in the season, when the kype grows and the general shape of the male becomes deeper and more slab-sided, a knowing angler who gets a good look at a fish can make a good guess at its sex. In rivers like the Miramichi there's a good chance that a grilse will be a male, but in many rivers that have a run made up almost entirely of grilse the ratio has to run about fifty-fifty. For all but a few anglers it will be next to impossible to determine the sex of the salmon they fish for before they are hooked or caught.

Peter uses much smaller flies, usually #10s or #12s for the females, and he fishes them at normal speeds with a conventional swing. He finds that while males are given to frequent movement and to resting at various places within their selected sphere, the females tend to choose a good lie and stick with it, just as most salmon do most of the time.

One would expect the females to be a better judge of a spawning area and more likely to make any territorial selection. The big females may have one or more suitors, including grilse and even parr, and for her to move to suit a suitor doesn't seem reasonable. During the angling season these fish are not yet engaged in spawning and have not yet come to the redds where they will join up to spawn. Perhaps the males become territorial on a temporary basis before the actual spawning takes place.

Peter tells of an instance where there were three males and a female lying together in a pool. All the males were caught before the female could be taken. There may be, he suggests, a protective measure to the territoriality as fall approaches.

How much territoriality exists in males I do not know and can only guess, but it does open up an interesting line of thinking. McElligott's experience should indicate to most of us that in late season especially we should cover the field and fish both small flies normally and large flies fast. It will be interesting to note which sex we catch on each method and if the percentages change between early season and late.

Of more importance to most anglers is the choice of flies to take large salmon as compared to grilse. Looking back over a great many years I can say with certainty that my most effective fly for big fish is the Surface Stonefly which is somewhat similar, when fished dry, to the more recent Bomber and, when fished wet, to the Muddler.

Many a time I've fished over a group of salmon made up predominantly of grilse and taken one of the big fish rather than a grilse on that fly. My reasoning is that the stonefly has a stronger imprint on the salmon's mind as a parr than other insects do and is therefore more likely to trigger a response in a big fish which has had a longer sea period to forget his stream preferences than the grilse have.

It has been my experience that with wet flies the drab patterns are more likely to take big salmon than the bright, flashy flies like the Silver Doctor. I do not consciously fish my flies differently for big salmon than for small ones. There may be something in a certain speed or swing of wet fly or a certain length of dry-fly draft that is particularly appealing to big salmon but, if so, I have yet to determine it. It is something a fisherman can amuse himself with and keep records on; one day we may know more about this part of salmon fishing than we do now.

When fishing dry I do like to work over big fish with a big fly like a #4 White Wulff. Here again it may be that it takes something larger to trigger the rise response in a salmon that has been at sea for two years or longer than it does for the one-year-sea-feeding fish. I find the Skater one of my better flies to interest big fish. That may be, too, that the extra excitement of its motion may trigger a response from the big fish that are longer away from parr feeding.

If, on only slight evidence, we begin to fish one way more than or exclusive of all others, we will miss out on a lot of fish that might have been more receptive to a different presentation. Only an impartial testing will give us reliable results. This is particularly true when an angler fishes several different rivers. Each river is different and so are its salmon.

[1979]

CHAPTER TWENTY-THREE

THE WULFF FLIES

*L*ee Wulff will be remembered for many things in the years ahead but will probably be best known for his series of Wulff dry-fly patterns, which, as he was fond of pointing out, aren't really specific patterns but rather a general kind of dry fly. The Wulff flies are more than sixty years old at this writing, and in that time have become standards with anglers worldwide. They're not just for salmon, either, and are perhaps most widely used as trout flies. They work, too, for steelhead, bass, panfish and just about any other gamefish that sometimes takes its food from the water's surface. Here is a history of those flies plus tying instructions from their originator.

IN THE WINTER of 1929–30 when I first developed the Wulff flies, it was a time for experimenting. Ed Hewitt had come up with the Spider, which was immediately popular with the small group of trout fishermen who had gone to small hooks on their flies. Hewitt had also given us the Bivisible, which floated readily and high on the water while the other flies of the day did not. Bivisibles caught fish more consistently than any other pattern, it seemed.

I looked at the dry flies available at the time and found that they were always slim-bodied and sparsely hackled, They were made only of feathers, and they were hard to keep afloat. If a fish were caught on one of them, the fly had to be retired to dry a while before it would float again.

I wanted a buggier-looking, heavier-bodied fly, and I needed more flotation in order to keep it up. I had in mind the big gray drakes that came out on New York's Ausable, which were heavier in the body than any of the dry-fly imitations of the day. Looking for a material that would float such a body, I came up with bucktail. The tail of the fly was most important since it would support the bend of the hook, where most of the weight is concentrated. Bucktail would make a much better tailing material than the conventional feather fibers because of its floating qualities and its strength. The flotation of the old flies was mostly at the front, and the usual wisps of feather fibers wouldn't make a strong, floating tail. For example, the few golden pheasant tippet-feather fibers of a Royal Coachman tail certainly didn't have enough strength to hold the hook bend up for very long.

Out of this thinking came the Gray Wulff, White Wulff and Royal Wulff. My use of bucktail was the first use of animal hair on dry flies. The Royal Wulff made the old, difficult-to-float but beautiful Royal Coachman pattern into a hell of a fly. The White Wulff was tied to imitate the coffin mayfly. I tied it both conventionally and with spent wings and no hackle to match the flies of the spinner fall—when the mayflies, spent with mating, fall to the water with wings outspread. Had I been brighter I would have patented the use of animal hair on dry flies and made some money, but I feel lucky that through these flies my name achieved a permanent place in fly-fishing.

The Gray Wulff has brown bucktail wings and tail, blue-gray hackles and a gray angora yarn (spun rabbit's fur) body. The White Wulff has white bucktail wings and tail, badger hackles and cream-colored angora for the body. The Royal Wulff has white bucktail wings, a brown bucktail tail, dark brown hackles and a body of red silk floss between two segments of wound peacock herl.

Dan Bailey, a close friend and one of my early fishing companions, insisted that I call the Gray Wulff by its present name instead of the Ausable Gray as I had thought to call it. It was Dan, who was beginning to tie and sell flies at that time, who sat down with me while we worked out the other patterns of the series to cover the field of trout-stream insects in general. The Grizzly Wulff, the Black Wulff, the Brown Wulff and the Blonde Wulff came out of those sessions.

Those first days and weeks of trying out the Wulff flies were a dream. I put on a Gray Wulff while fishing the Salmon River with Dan Bailey near Malone, New York, and I caught fifty-one trout with the same fly without once having to take it from the leader, which was a fantastic feat at the time. I used Mucilin line grease as a fly floatant instead of the universally used mixture of paraffin dissolved in benzene or gasoline, into which the fly was dipped. I found I could catch five or six trout between greasings, and I was glad I had secured the fly so well with lacquer when I tied it. Anything that makes fishing simpler and lets me spend more time with my fly on the water and less time in fussing with things to get ready or while on the stream makes me happier.

I used many kinds of hairs for the tails and wings of these flies. I even bought some "Chinese" bucktails that were small and the color of red fox fur and used the material for the Wulff flies. It worked very well. I tried other hairs (I failed to try calftail back in the early days of testing) and decided that bucktail gave the best flotation and durability to the flies. Calftail, while it does not have quite the elegance of bucktail, has great floating properties, and it is a lot easier to match into proper wing lengths and work into proper spreads, or positioning, of the wings.

My original instincts had been right. I had felt that a heavier-bodied fly—I used flies tied on #10 hooks mostly—would be more attractive to the trout than the slim-bodied, small patterns of the day. The trout would be able to see it from a greater depth, and it would seem to them like a bigger mouthful and something that was worth coming up for. It might even look at a quick glance like some strange terrestrial: a bee, a wasp or a fluttering moth. Part of my deep feeling was that if it looked like a bug—if it had a familiar look to the trout—whether identical to the mayfly or not, it would draw rises.

Soon after the Wulff flies began to gain popularity, Dan Bailey started to go to Montana in the summers to fish. Because he taught science at Brooklyn Polytechnical Institute for a living, Dan had his summers free to fish. Preston Jennings, a great student of stream insects, was writing a book about insects and trout flies. Dan showed him the Wulff flies when they fished together in Montana, saying he was tying a lot of them to sell and was catching a lot of fish on them. Preston looked at them and said they imitated no insects, and he couldn't believe that they were actually good trout flies. Although the Montana fishing convinced Preston that they would take fish, he didn't put them in his well-known *A Book of Trout Flies,* published in 1935. He told me he couldn't figure out why trout liked them so well. It was, he said, one of the unreasonable things about trout fishing.

To tie the Wulff, begin the thread near the hook eye, wind down the shank to the bend and return back up the shank to the start. At this point, lacquer may be applied to give a good bond between the thread and hook shank, which will prevent the twisting of thread and materials as the fly is tied. Select bucktail to be used for the tail, and match the fine ends of the hair so they are as even as possible. This can be done by pulling out the longer hairs and resetting them so they are even with the tips of the others or by placing the hairs in a narrow container, such as a cartridge shell, and tapping the container gently on the tabletop. Hair-evening tools for fly-tying are also available for this purpose.

Place the tail along the hook shank with the tips extending beyond the bend of the hook. Wrap the thread down to the bend of the hook. Wrap the thread down to the bend of the hook, and clip off the excess hair near the eye of the hook. Apply a drop of lacquer to the thread wraps along the hook shank; the lacquer will penetrate to the hook and also remain on the thread to help set the angora-wool body tightly when it is applied in the next step. Good setting of the body makes for long life in a fly.

Tie in a length of angora wool at the head and wrap the thread to the bend and back to the head. Wrap the angora wool forward, forming the proper shape of body, and tie it off at the head. As you are winding the angora, also rotate the material to avoid twisting it, forming a smooth body.

Select the bucktail to be used for the wings and even the tips in the same manner that you evened the tips of the bucktail used for the tail. (If calftail is used for the wings, the evening process is not necessary.) Lay the bucktail over the shank with the tips facing forward over the hook eye. Tie the hair in, then bring the thread in front of the wings and make them stand up vertically by building up a wall of thread in front of the bucktail. By splitting the hair into two wings and winding between and around at the base, the wings are set into the right position. A drop or two of lacquer should be applied between the wings at their base. The lacquer will penetrate the hair and thread and set the wings securely to the hook. The lacquer should still be soft as the hackles are wound, which will set the hackle fibers securely in place. Saddle hackles, which I prefer, are usually strong of fiber but without great strength where the fibers join the hackle stem. Setting their bases in lacquer makes a durable fly.

Two long saddle hackles are used for the standard Wulff. After you tie them in, bring the first one back between the wings and wind it around the shank close behind the wings until it is just long enough to pass between the two upright wings again. Bring it between the wings and hold it at the hook eye between your forefinger and thumb. Wind the second hackle around the shank in front of the wings to the hackle's tip. Wrap the tying thread over the two hackle tips, trim excess, whip-finish and lacquer the head.

Of course there are many versions of the Wulff flies. I've seen them with the wings slanted forward, and I've seen them with the wings slanted backward. I've even read a short article in a minor publication by a man I've never met or corresponded with entitled, "The Right Way to Tie the Wulff Flies." But all this is good, because the Wulff fly is a category of flies, not an inflexible pattern.

I tie the Wulff flies in a variety of patterns. On #10, #12, #14 or #16 hooks, with slimmer-than-usual bodies and wings and sometimes with less winds of hackle, I use them to imitate the Hendricksons when those flies are on the water. On a very long-shanked hook, with a slim body and long tail, the Wulff fly looks like a small dragonfly. On very large and heavy hooks, when the hackles aren't big enough or strong enough to give proper flotation, I tie a clipped-deerhair body to float the big fly.

One of my variations is the Scraggly. It floats even higher than the standard Wulff, and it has a bulkier body. It is, perhaps, a better imitation of a nondescript, dying terrestrial than the standard Wulff.

The Scraggly is tied by using chenille or another bulky body material and winding a hackle palmer-style down the body. The body and hackle add bulk and flotation at the same time. The Grizzly Scraggly is a Gray Wulff with a grizzly hackle wound over a chenille body; the Bumble Bee Scraggly is a Gray Wulff that has a chenille body of alternating yellow and black with a badger hackle wound over it to replace the gray body of the Gray Wulff; the White Moth Scraggly is a White Wulff that has a cream chenille body with a badger hackle palmer tied over it. These Scragglies float high and attract attention from hungry fish deep in the water because of the size of their bodies.

I use Wulff flies for bass as well as for trout and salmon. In

#4 or larger they have considerable bulk and will attract bass, yet they are lighter to cast than the average-size bass bugs. Heavily hackled with a clipped-deerhair body, they can be jumped across the surface a bit from time to time to make them even more attractive to the bass.

Of course, as I was originally dealing with a mayfly imitation, I tried out a single wing as well as the split wings. I made up a few dozen flies with a wing that consisted of a single tuft of bucktail, either vertical or slanting back at an angle like a mayfly's wings. It seemed that I had just as many rises to the single-wing versions as I did to the split-wing versions. I was especially successful with the single-wing Royal Wulff. But since I was poor at the time, as was almost everyone else during those Depression days, I tied and promoted the Wulff flies the way my customers wanted them—with split wings. But, while I feel that single-wing flies are better imitations than are split wings, divided wings do give better flotation and are more visible to the angler. And the illusion the split-wing Wulffs create seems completely adequate.

When fishing fast water I like Wulff flies with quite bushy wings and sometimes as many as three hackles. They should be tied in this manner so they ride high and don't drown in the rough water. In very still water, I use either the bushy flies as terrestrial imitations or the more sparsely tied patterns as imitations of stream insects. I tie almost all of my flies in a wide variety of density of materials as well as in a wide variety of colors. My use of hackle may vary from the normally bushy to none at all, such as in a spinner pattern when the wings are spread out horizontally to imitate the mayfly's spent wings.

When tying spent-wing Wulffs with no hackle, I use the fine hairs from the tip end of the bucktail, and I flare these hairs out at the wings and at the tail to give maximum flotation with minimum visibility. These tip-end bucktail hairs are more wiry, and they have very fine diameters. They are stronger than the rest of the hairs on the bucktail. In this instance the bucktail is far superior to calftail. The color may be varied by dyeing, and the bodies may be tied thick or thin, depending upon the spinner being imitated. Most spinners have more slender bodies than the standard Wulff flies.

The Wulff flies will also serve as bulky, substitute Skaters when tied with the usual or a greater amount of hackle support and wing thickness. In 1933 a salmon fisherman on the Liscombe River in Nova Scotia to whom I'd given a Wulff to try reported good luck with it. I came to watch him fish because he was doing better than we were on the Ecum Secum River. I found him fishing the gift fly as a wet fly, dragging it across the surface of the pool below a falls. I hadn't explained to him when I gave him the fly how dry flies were fished, and apparently he had never fished with dry flies before. By fishing it just as he would a wet fly, he made it into a substitute Skater.

I tried the fly with a free float, and I failed to get a rise. It may have been because he'd caught all the takers with his dragging fly or because the salmon actually liked the dragged fly better than the free-floating fly. I don't know, because he had no rises while we both fished the pool. This is typical of the situations that leave you to wonder about the reasons salmon take a fly.

I have a letter somewhere in my files from Ken Lockwood, a fine fisherman and outdoor writer from New Jersey. He wrote me soon after Ray Bergman's *Trout* came out in 1938 and brought the Wulff flies to the notice of fishermen. Ken explained that he'd come up with a version of the Gray Wulff that had a clipped-deerhair body instead of the angora-wool body. It was being called the Irresistible. Did I mind? I wrote back to wish him well and say that I didn't mind.

Trout fishermen don't seem ready for categories of flies; instead they seem to stick by particular patterns. The Wulff flies, like Don Gapen's original Muddler Minnow, should be only the beginning—opening up new categories, systems or fields of flies for the trout fisherman. The clipped-deerhair fly head was the new and especially effective idea introduced by the Muddler; it should be tied not only with a tinsel body and turkey-feather wings, but in every conceivable combination of materials that make up flies. Similarly, the Gray Wulff was only the first fly in a new category for the fisherman.

The many techniques used to fish the Wulff flies and the many different insects the Wulff flies may imitate reflect that the flies are a category of patterns. The Wulff flies almost seem made to be tied in various patterns. I like to think of flies such as the Wulff as categories, in the same manner as trout and salmon form a category with the first name of *Salmo*.

[1980]

CHAPTER TWENTY-FOUR

FIFTY YEARS OF DRY-FLY SALMON

*T*his chapter was written about ten years ago [*1980*] *and might now be retitled "Sixty years . . . ." As I mentioned in this book's introduction, the longevity and breadth of Wulff's experience is without parallel among those who wrote about salmon fishing. Wulff didn't invent dry-fly salmon fishing, but he was certainly its foremost proponent over the years. Here's the sum of much of that experience: a first-rate primer on salmon and the dry fly.*

THE MOMENT WAS ETCHED so indelibly in my memory that even today, a half century later, I can see the silvery shape, the black spots on its gill covers, the slow drift through crystal water up to the surface to take the Grizzly Bivisible and the swift turn-away and leap when the hook sank home. The memory stays, although the Hut Pool on Nova Scotia's Margaree River, where that first salmon of mine took a dry fly, has disappeared with the river's meanderings. The intervening years have been filled with the rises of thousands of other Atlantic salmon.

That year, 1933, started me on a career of casting flies, preferably of the floating type, on the salmon rivers of the North Atlantic.

Dry-fly fishing for salmon was so new at the time that only two patterns were being used to any extent: the Pink Lady, which was George LaBranche's favorite, and the Bivisibles that Ed Hewitt had designed. My own dries of the Wulff series—high floaters with heavier than usual bodies and bucktail wings and tails—were more insectlike and they, the White Wulff in particular, would become the favored dry flies for salmon.

But their acceptance and that of surface flies for salmon in general didn't come overnight. I would give away my Wulff patterns to anglers I fished with and then, when I'd meet them again on the river a year later, I'd find the fly tucked away in a corner of their fly box where they'd put it the year before, pristine, unused. It is hard to believe how traditional the salmon anglers of that day were. Like Henry Ford, who believed that any color was fine for a car as long as it was black, salmon anglers seemed to feel that any fly was OK as long as it was a Jock Scott or one of their other very few trusted traditional wet flies. I used dry flies to bring delight and surprise to the anglers and guides I fished with, and my memories are filled with examples of their angling wonder.

Perhaps the best example was with Jack Young of Georges Bay, Newfoundland. Jack was the finest guide I have ever known. I watched and helped him build a log cabin on a salmon river without his using a single nail or any other hardware. His only tools were his axe and his hunting knife. When the cabin was finished it had walls of peeled spruce and fir logs, a leakproof roof of birch bark covered with sod that immediately started to grow, a door that swung on wooden pins, and four bunks well mattressed with spruce bough tips. Jack was a most courteous man and thoroughly knowledgeable about Newfoundland's hunting and fishing. Besides all that, he could make the finest English muffin–type biscuits that ever came from a campfire.

Jack had never seen a dry fly fished before he guided me on the Serpentine River in 1940. He started out as a disbeliever, then became a convert.

Jack stood beside me on our last day as I fished the Governor's Pool, working over a large salmon we had seen porpoise there a few minutes before. His eyes were on my dry-fly floats as doggedly as were my own. That salmon's first rise was a test of my maturity as a dry-fly angler and, fortunately, I passed it. The big White Wulff had floated time after time over the salmon's lie. Suddenly we saw him materialize under it . . . saw the white of his open mouth and followed the head-and-tail rise through its deliberate pattern. But I saw, too, that although he opened his mouth as the fly came near, the fly was still floating and passing his eye as his mouth closed. My arm was tense, cocked to lift the rod and set the hook, but I held it still and let the fly drift on to drown in the wash of the swirl his tail made as he sank to his lie again.

Had I whipped the fly away from the salmon's head as it drifted by, I'm sure he would never have risen again. But a few casts later he did, and this time I could see the white fly disappear into his mouth and his jaws close. He was a wild fish, a big male that leaped and leaped, twenty-two times in all, before he came to the tailer and warmed our hearts with the dry fly's success. It was then that Jack Young stated succinctly what many of us have felt over the years.

"Mr. Wulff," he said, "I don't think there's anything more beautiful in all the world than a salmon's rise to a dry fly."

Then there was Sam Shinnix of River of Ponds. It was 1941, and that isolated spot—Sam and his family made up more than half the souls in the town—had seen few salmon fishermen except for the Royal Navy officers who came to fish on their time off when their ships were near and a few anglers from Hawke Bay, which had its own two salmon rivers, nine miles down the shore. Sam was the patriarch of River of Ponds, the political boss if politics there were, the best fiddler at the square dances, the best salmon fisherman and the head guide.

He became my guide, for he had first whack at any job that developed in his bailiwick. He was a positive man, infallible in the eyes of his peers. He was a canny man, too, and when I took out a #4 White Wulff to tie on my leader, his face took on a shocked expression. Then he laughed. "They'd as soon take a sea gull, sir," was his comment.

I handed Sam the fly and he looked at it curiously. "You mean it, sir?" he asked. "You're going to fish with that?" He laughed again as if humoring a small boy.

We moved to the head of the tidal pool just above his house. Later I was to have fishing camps on that river and would come to know it well. It rose in the high, rocky and barren country in the middle of Newfoundland's northern peninsula. The salmon liked dry flies well enough when the water was normal or in low flow, but it was hard to bring a salmon to a dry fly when the river was high and dark and stained with the peat-bog drainoffs. The river, though dropping, was high—and still as dark as bitter tea.

A silvery sixteen-pounder rolled to the surface just above where we stopped to fish. I began casting the big White Wulff over him. The sun was low and conditions were, I thought, ideal. The fish rolled up again between two casts but for twenty minutes ignored the fly. Then we saw the silver of his side as he came up under the fly; but he didn't break the surface.

Encouraged, I continued casting for another twenty minutes without a response. The cook from our launch came up to say that supper was ready to go on the table. I made a few desperation casts, and on the last one as the fly passed over the salmon's back for some strange reason I twitched the rod, sank the fly, and let it drift on, a white blur just under the surface. There was a great splash and the salmon was hooked.

"There's some live rocks out there," Sam yelled. "Don't let him get to the far side!"

But the warning came too late. The fish reached the submerged rocks, passed between two of them and headed back toward the sea, snapping the leader and leaping derisively immediately afterward.

I think Sam was more surprised that the salmon took that "God-awful thing" underwater—where everyone *knew* you needed one of the standard English patterns to catch a fish—than if he had taken it from the surface. I was nearly as surprised as Sam at the maneuver that had drawn the rise. From that time I have never left a reluctant fish without dunking the fly over his back for an underwater drift. Salmon have made some gymnastic rises to reach my fly from that position. It seems to surprise them, as much as that first wild rise surprised Sam and me.

The next day five grilse and two good salmon were caught on that big white fly and Sam Shinnix was converted.

A host of memories of the River of Ponds in normal flow crowd in on me as I write. Once I climbed out on a big rock in the middle of one of the upper pools. I slid up from the downstream side and, as I got to my knees, I saw two salmon move away upstream from the area just above the rock. I moved up and sat on the rock's upstream face, feet dangling in the flow.

I began to cast to the good-looking spots within range, working each one carefully and covering the water with several flies. No salmon rose to my offerings but, as I glanced down to see how I would slide off the rock and wade on upstream, I saw that one of the salmon had returned to his previous lie. I watched the fish while continuing to make my fifty-foot casts. Finally, I let my line swing around downstream and reeled in until my leader was halfway into the guides. Slowly I swung the rod forward and danced the fly on the surface. The third time my fly touched the water the salmon lifted up and took it.

Salmon are gifted with amazing speed. Even though I was

watching that fish closely, at a distance of not more than eight feet, his move was so fast that he had taken the fly before I realized he'd left his position near the streambed.

This bit of learning has stood me in good stead many times since. Now, in clear rivers, especially the larger ones, when I wade deep or fish from a canoe, I'll drop anchor or take a wading position and then look carefully over all the water I can see. When I spot fish that are reasonably close I purposely ignore them while first fishing farther water where I think salmon may lie. After fifteen minutes or more, when the fish have accepted my presence as something harmless that drifted down the river and took hold there, I start to fish for the closest salmon. They're used to my presence and my casting action, whereas a cast over them when I first arrived would have had no chance of success.

I drop a big fly over a salmon's head and watch for a reaction. If in the first few casts he shows any sign of interest or moves at all as the fly passes over him, I change to a smaller fly and drift that down to him. Very often the smaller fly will bring a rise. If it doesn't, I go back to the big fly then vary my presentation through a number of dry-fly categories and sizes. It is rare when such a salmon moves at all under the fly that he cannot be brought to the fly. All casts must be careful, all movements smooth and easy. Because the fish is close and visible it is possible to make each cast perfect and to make sure your fly has drifted beyond his vision or point of interest before it is picked up for the next presentation.

It was on the upper River of Ponds at about a four-foot depth that I found one of my most memorable dry-fly salmon. The fish had risen to my fly while I was casting my way up through the pool. I knew by the character of the rise that it was a good fish.

I moved closer to his lie. At about thirty-five feet I guessed that I could see him: a dark shadow lying over some dark rocks. My position was dead across the current, a spot from which I would be able to see him best, from which the casting would take a minimum of effort and where my line and leader would not come nearer to him than the fly. I didn't feel I'd come close enough to alarm him, and after a few minutes I continued casting, using a Gray Wulff #8, the same fly to which he had originally risen.

For almost two hours we played a game, that salmon and I. I'd long before learned never to strike till I was sure as I could be that my fly was inside the salmon's mouth. Within a dozen casts he came up again. I watched his long silvery shape move up under the fly; I saw his nose break the surface and come up out of the water with my fly riding on top of it; then I watched as he slid back downward to let the fly float on a foot or two behind him before I lifted it out of the water.

Then he ignored the fly. A few casts with a White Wulff brought him up again for another look. He turned down again without breaking the surface and the fly danced on the little push waves he made. Then he showed no more interest in that fly.

A Surface Stonefly, usually my ace-in-the-hole, was next. The salmon came up under the first float, allowed the fly to pass over and sank it precisely with a well-aimed flick of his tail. Then quiet again.

A Gray Wulff drifted over him again brought another close look with as many as fifteen investigative rises until finally he paid no attention to any flies. There were other salmon to fish for. I knew his location, and I thought it might be wise to let him rest until later in the evening.

Before I left I followed another of my "rules" or patterns of salmon fishing: I put the original Gray Wulff over him again in as near a replica as I could of the cast that brought the first rise. I make it a point never to leave a fish that has risen but not been pricked without one last cast or two with the fly that triggered the first rise. I had little hope he'd take it; the cast and the effort were perfunctory. I dropped the fly just over his nose. Up he came, pushing his big head half out of the water to take it. He was a good fish, about twenty pounds. More than that, he was the most interesting dry-fly salmon I'd ever fished for.

A beginning Atlantic salmon fisherman's greatest dilemma can be knowing when to set the hook while fishing with a dry fly. He knows that he must set the hook for his line is slack to the dry fly and salmon taking it will rarely hook themselves. If he is an accomplished trout fisherman the dilemma may be even greater than normal. The thing that throws most anglers off— if they aren't sharp-eyed, cool, calm and collected—is that, in the excitement, they are *sure* the salmon has come to take their fly. He's a swift, sure fish: Why should he miss it?

They strike, and the fly comes sailing back to them untouched.

Naturally, many an angler is hurried by his excitement at seeing so large a fish coming to the fly and doesn't wait long enough for the salmon to close his mouth on it. Others are so paralyzed by their excitement they fail to strike until the fish has ejected the fly. But many, many times the fish did not actually take the fly. He may come up for just a look, and that look may bring him within a couple of feet, a foot or just a few inches.

Advice to a trout fisherman is usually to strike deliberately, as he would with a big brown trout. How big is big? How many have really hooked and caught five-pound trout or better on a dry fly? There is only one time to strike and that is when the salmon takes the fly out of sight into his mouth—or the fly goes out of sight in splashing or swirling water and you *think* it's in his mouth. Striking well with the dry fly requires an intentness and control few anglers have developed, and even the wisest must puzzle now and then over why he failed to hook a salmon.

I had one like that on the Grand Cascapedia in Quebec recently.

We had anchored the canoe close to a very large salmon, fished the far-away fish for fifteen minutes before casting to him. He lay in a slight depression with a fish half his size some ten feet closer to us. A Bomber over him made him move. The next ten casts passing over left him unmoved.

I changed to a Surface Stonefly, and on the first cast he came savagely to the fly, jaws agape, spray flying. I lifted the rod, and the fly sailed back through the air over my head. I still don't know why I failed to hook that salmon.

I think it is wise to rest a fish a bit after a particularly vicious rise so, without thinking much about it, I let my next cast drop the fly well short of the big fish but, as it happened, close enough to the smallest salmon. He rose deliberately and took the fly. Reflecting on it later, I should have taken the fly away from the smaller fish. After I'd landed that ten pounder, moving the canoe to a shore eddy to do it, we went back to the same anchorage. But the large salmon—which I'm sure could have been coaxed into another rise after a suitable wait—was no longer there.

One of my finest dry-fly memories came on the River Dee in Scotland where George LaBranche had tried and failed to bring a salmon to the dry fly, although Arthur H. E. Wood, who owned the water, was catching them by the dozens on his famous greased-line method with wet flies. I was there to fish competitively with "Jock Scott" (pen name of Donald Rudd), premier salmon-fishing writer of Britain. It was my six-foot, one-and-three-quarters-ounce split cane against his sixteen-and-a-half-foot greenheart; he had indicated that my rod was a toy rather than a capable fishing tool. I was there to prove it wasn't. I caught one more fish than he did, and that fish took a dry fly.

The night before, Captain Tommy Edwards, longtime British casting champ, had stopped by our hotel. After looking at my rod he declared it wouldn't cast sixty feet ("twenty yards" as he put it) and wouldn't even reach most salmon. He was standing on the bank when I cast out a #8 White Wulff. Seeing the rise he cried: "Hah! A sea trout."

But it proved to be a salmon of ten pounds, one that hadn't read the book that British salmon don't take dry flies.

What about dry flies in the rain? Will salmon take them? They will! They will! I've taken a good many dry-fly salmon in the rain. The clincher was back in 1946 one August evening on the Lower Humber. I was waist-deep in a swift and steady flow at Shellbird Island Pool. No salmon were moving. I had fished a #8 Gray Wulff for half an hour without response. I'd seen one fish leap as I walked down to the pool, so I knew there was at least one salmon in the water I was fishing.

It began to sprinkle. A few drops, big drops, far apart, and I put on my rain jacket. I switched to a #4 White Wulff, something easier for both the salmon and myself to see against the dark water under a darkening sky. By the time I had made the fly change, the storm was sweeping over the limestone cliffs that facade the river. Thunder roared and lightning flashed. Rain pelted down so heavily I could barely make out the white fly at the end of a fifty-foot cast. Rain ran down my neck. It soaked my casting arm up to the elbow and collected there. I thought to myself: "You darn fool—you haven't got sense enough to go in out of the rain!"

Then a big Humber salmon came up under my fly in a dramatic rise. His head came up out of the water followed by half his body. I set the hook and half an hour later had a thirty-pounder lying on the grass of the shore. I was thoroughly soaked and thoroughly happy. That fish has since given me hope and kept me fishing through weather that would have driven me ashore before the Humber experience.

Is a fine leader necessary for the fishing of a dry fly? I like to use one. It makes me feel I'm separating my fly from me as much as possible, and I feel quite comfortable in playing salmon on leaders of six-pound test. But heavy leaders do catch fish. The first year I fished Newfoundland, 1935, I watched my friend Vic Coty make the sloppiest cast I'd ever seen him make. His big dry fly popped down in a tangled mess of line and leader. A twenty-pounder, our largest of that trip, rose up into the mess, took his fly and hooked himself.

Nothing is impossible or even improbable in salmon fishing. Still, I pattern myself on the basis of my experiences and fish according to certain precepts. I never forget that each salmon has a mind of its own and can be most unorthodox and contrary.

When I flew down to Newfoundland in 1947 with my J3 Piper Cub on floats, it was the first nongovernment, nonmilitary plane to be based there. I could fly back into the wild country of that island and Labrador where no one had ever fished for salmon before and find fabulous fishing. One of those places was the inlet to Big Blue Lake. I came over it on a sunny afternoon at about 750 feet and looked down at the inlet and the shallow water around it with an eye for salmon. The water was only lightly peat-stained, and from that altitude I could see rocks and large things on the bottom. I looked for individual salmon but saw none. There were a couple of long, dark rock ledges stretching out from the mouth; I made a mental note that they would probably be slippery if I waded out on them.

I circled to look for any obstacles that might interfere with my landing or taxiing into shore. As the plane's shadow crossed the ledges, my heart came up into my throat. The ledges disintegrated into hundreds of salmon that scattered in all directions. There were more Atlantic salmon there than I'd ever seen in one place. I circled again, landed and taxied to shore. I wore waders when I flew and my six-foot rod was always set up in the plane beside me. I slipped into my vest and waded carefully out through the shallows to the area where the "ledges" had been.

There was no wind. The lake was mirror still. Breaking the surface here and there were little black triangles which, as I drew closer, I could identify as the tips of salmon's tails. They hardly moved which meant that the fish were hanging just below the surface in a slightly head-down attitude. I moved out with the slight flow of the incoming water so as to send out a minimum of wading-waves. The rod as I'd taken it from its hangers in the plane carried a dry fly at the end of the leader—a #6 White Wulff, my searching fly. I cast five feet in front of the nearest tail. The fly dropped gently and a tail disappeared. I waited, not moving the fly. I set the hook and the salmon raced away amid the swirls and splashes of that great spreading school.

I brought him to where I stood, knee deep, and picked him up by the tail. He would weigh about twelve pounds: a trim and beautiful fish. I worked the hook free and slid him back into the lake. One after another I caught salmon from the school, never changing my fly. Sometimes I made it twitch when I became impatient, but it didn't seem to make much difference. I just cast it out and let it lie most of the time. There were so many salmon there I don't believe *any* fly could have landed without being in sight of at least one. I caught a dozen fish, releasing them all. And then, satisfied, I flew back to camp. (Had I stayed, I think I might have caught a hundred.)

Several times that year I took special friends there to fish, and each time the number of catchable fish seemed endless. Sometimes on dead calm days the drifting tails were there to see. Those salmon were making their endless wait for spawning time, and I believe most of them spawned at the mouth, in the great gravel bar that spread around it, as the inlet was small and a quarter of the fish would have filled it. The country was opening up. The paper company was making roads; word of the concentration of fish leaked out. The inlet could be reached by dogsled over an early snow, and spawning salmon were often killed for dog food. It could also be reached by long portages up the river and through its chain of lakes. In a year or two there were only a very few salmon where there had been so many. How glad I am to have seen it when I did.

Perhaps the most exciting dry-fly fishing of all is the attempt for big salmon with the smallest of dry flies. In 1964 a group of us decided to try for a salmon of more than twenty pounds on a #16. In order to tie the biggest possible fly on a #16 hook I designed the Prefontaine. It is essentially a Bivisible with a long bucktail snoot and a tail of its own hackle tips. The snoot makes it flop and wobble when skated on the surface in retrieve, the only fly I know that has an action of its own. To see a salmon of over twenty pounds charge such a tiny fly is a sight to remember.

Only a few anglers have taken Atlantic salmon of twenty pounds or more on a single #16 hook. One lucky afternoon on the Moisie two great fish, each weighing in at twenty-four pounds, took my Prefontaine five casts apart and were brought in to where I could hand-tail and carry them ashore.

The playing of so great a fish on so small a fly calls for sensitivity and judgment. Size sixteen hooks either break or bend at a pull of four pounds; the fine wire can cut through flesh on even a four-pound pressure. Most big fish on such small hooks are lost because of tactical errors early in the struggle. A little too much pressure at the start can slightly loosen the hook's hold. Then, in the final moments of playing, the already weakened flesh gives away.

I have a feeling when playing an over-twenty-pounder on a #16 that I can sense the varying urgency in his runs and leaps, and I do my best to accommodate him with suitable pressure or lack of it. I must urge him on when I can handle his runs and try to coax him into relaxing when I cannot and need time to reposition. It is almost as if I must sense his heartbeats and measure constantly his remaining strength. It is a challenge worthy of the finest fishermen; those who succeed enter a charmed circle of salmon anglers.

After fifty years of experience I have found there is no fishing in the world quite like dry-fly fishing for Atlantic salmon. Not all salmon will take a dry fly well, particularly those in Europe. Fortunately, most of the salmon of this continent's rivers are as addicted to dry flies as the anglers are, and that makes for wonderful sport.

[1983]

CHAPTER TWENTY-FIVE

WHAT MAKES SALMON RISE TO THE FLY

*O*f all the salmon that enter a particular river, only some of them will ever rise to an angler's fly. This has led me to wonder often that if every fly-caught salmon were then killed, would fishermen then be selectively breeding a strain of salmon that never took flies at all? This hasn't happened yet, but it's theoretically possible. Salmon and many other fish are genetically plastic, which means their populations respond relatively quickly in evolutionary ways to many environmental (and man-made) influences. As such, salmon are the subject of intensive and expensive genetic research. Wulff argues persuasively here that perhaps that research money would be better spent on saving salmon and their habitat first, before the subject of that research disappears altogether.

·········

THAT AN ATLANTIC SALMON occasionally takes a fly is a wonderful thing. Our salmon fishing is founded on this paradox: A fish incapable of digesting food takes something he cannot eat as if he intended to eat it. The incidence of a salmon rising to a fly is rare compared to the rising of a fish, such as a trout, trying to maintain its strength or seeking nourishment. Certain salmon may never rise to a fly during their entire spawning run; others, particularly the grilse, will rise quite freely.

Why, then, does an Atlantic salmon rise to a fly?

When a salmon returns to his stream after his sea-feeding sojourn, he has behind him more years of stream living and stream memories than he has of sea-feeding time. Most of us believe that the memories of his stream life are the most important factor in his inclination to take a fly. We know that grilse, which enjoy the greatest proportion of stream life, rise more freely than the larger salmon, which feed longer in the ocean and are twice as removed in time from their stream-feeding memories. The insect-feeding period of the salmon's life is usually longer; for the grilse, however, it is more recent by at least a year, and so, perhaps, his stream-feeding memories are more vivid and influential.

Let us look for a moment at the Pacific salmon, whose stream-life period and stream insect-feeding period as parr are much shorter than the Atlantic salmon's.

Pacifics, which often feed on plankton rather than insects, rise to our insectlike Atlantic salmon flies very poorly. To be sure, other factors are involved, but the stream life of the Atlantic salmon seems to be the key to their taking a man-made appetizer for which they have no alimentary need.

Traditionally, Atlantic salmon flies have been imitations of winged insects, even though we fish them underwater. Dry flies, nymphlike forms, tube flies and the like have gained in prominence, along with the idea that anything related to a parr's stream diet will interest a salmon. Last year I broke with tradition and fished with imitations of terrestrials that might be blown or hop to a stream's surface. My most successful fly was an ant: a regular component of a parr's environment and diet. The most successful range of Atlantic salmon flies, despite our efforts at expansion, seems to be limited by the parr's natural types of food.

How do we transfer this instinct to take a fly into our future planning for the Atlantic salmon? If we take away their stream life and raise them in tanks, feeding them only fish-food pellets, will that, in time, affect their inclination to rise to our artificial flies? Will they, like the pellet-fed trout in my ponds, show no interest in insects but avidly take pellets and pellet imitations? The whole spectrum of our research for Atlantic salmon deserves careful scrutiny.

Ask any salmon angler, "How do you rate the Atlantic salmon as a gamefish?" and he's likely to respond, "At the top!" If that's true, and most of us believe it is, why are we trying to change him? And, if we do decide to change him, should we not ensure that he does not lose any of the attributes that make him our favorite fish? Must we not be certain that in our effort to "improve" him we do not lose his instinct to leap high or take a fly? Are we willing to let him become like a Pacific salmon in his risings in order to make him grow faster, as Pacific salmon do?

Geneticists will tell you that when you change one characteristic of a species it will almost certainly affect others. In the hatchery breeding of brook trout for stocking, the genetic objective was a disease-free, fast-growing fish that would gain maximum weight for the food it ate. The fish with these qualities were saved and bred, the others discarded. The result was the development of a fast-growing, food-efficient, relatively disease-free strain . . . but one of those discarded traits was the capacity for long life. The new strain self-destructed at three years of age.

In our zeal to genetically engineer the ideal salmon strain, we must monitor to ensure that where certain traits are to be gained others not be lost.

Our salmon are a great gamefish. Why, then, are we spending money on genetic research at a point when our overriding fear is that we will lose them altogether—through poor management, poaching, illegal or over-heavy harvest? Would it not be wiser to spend our money now on solving the problems of poaching, excessive and uncontrolled Indian take, mismanagement or over-harvest on migrations in the sea?

Anglers like the salmon the way they are. We appreciate that each river's salmon are different and that the biological research should proceed in recognition of the uniqueness of each river's stock. We believe that studying the protected, force-fed fish in hatcheries to find out how wild fish react is like studying people on welfare to find out how business people operate. Force-fed hatchery trout will give us few clues as to how wild fish survive in their highly competitive environment.

On the other side of the coin are the commercial fishermen. They do not like the Atlantic salmon the way it is. They want it to grow faster, spend less time in the streams, become increasingly food-efficient. *This* is the sort of research that can be done in a hatchery or rearing station—by selective breeding, salmon can be developed that mature faster and grow fatter than pigs! Whether or not these salmon ever rise to a fly or jump is of no concern. Such traits, in terms of the profits of salmon ranching, are expendable.

The commercial sector argues that if salmon can be raised profitably in pens or by ranching, the market will soon be saturated: the price of salmon will go down, and poaching will no longer be worthwhile. Is this plausible? Since the *raison d'etre* of the commercial fishing industry is to make money, they will certainly control the market. Should the market price of salmon plummet, the supply will be withheld until demand pushes it up again—the effort being to keep the price of salmon as high as possible. Cheap salmon on the market is a pipe dream, and poaching will remain as tempting as ever.

As anglers, our problem is not only to secure good management and good protection for the salmon but to promote viable research. Research must be conducted river by river, to build and improve the stocks, protecting those stocks from the losses they are now suffering. We must put a stop to the slaughter of our best breeding stock—which leaves only the runts (grilse) as progenitors of future stocks—via the commercial food fisheries. The commercial quota on the Miramichi recently was 3,000 grilse and 12,000 salmon!

Grilse are not "young" salmon that will automatically grow into big ones. Grilse are often as old as the ten or twenty pounders they accompany in the same run, and their chances of survival for a second run hover near one in five. No cattleman would consider breeding his runts and slaughtering his best bulls and cows for hamburger, but the government's salmon policy does just that.

Research and river-by-river management appear to be our wisest course. Iceland has eliminated netting in the sea, manages each river individually and even uses fly-caught fish as hatchery breeders, in order to perpetuate the inclination to rise to a fly. Can we not do it, too?

We must let no river be depleted of its native stock. We must work to permit the most aggressive, the fastest and the fiercest of each river's salmon to survive and to flourish. We must fish for our salmon and keep them the way they are, resisting the attempts to sublimate their superb and matchless characteristics for a homogenized and domesticated species. If the salmon remains a high-leaping, swift-running, unique fighting fish that takes a fly, stands at the top of the gamefish list and contributes in both dollars and sport, where is the man who does not benefit?

[1983]

CHAPTER TWENTY-SIX

GAMEFISH STATUS FOR ATLANTIC SALMON

M*any people are surprised to learn that the Atlantic salmon in Canada isn't protected strictly as a gamefish. It's been well demonstrated that the value derived from salmon as a sport-fish is many times the value of the commercial salmon fishery, and protection of wild salmon stocks through gamefish status seems eminently logical. But the commercial fishing interests have managed to persist politically.*

This article was written in 1989 for The Atlantic Salmon Jour-nal, *which is the official magazine of the Atlantic Salmon Fed-eration, an international group that's worked on behalf of salmon conservation for many years and which for many years had been spearheaded often by Lee Wulff. Here Wulff attempts to con-*

vince both his fellow ASF members and the general public to throw their political weight behind the gamefish question. His effort met with surprisingly little success. He does have my vote; with your reading of this chapter, I hope he'll get yours.

WE ARE SAVING the Atlantic salmon. It is part of a national pattern in the U.S. and Canada. Our record of losing the species we love in Canada and the U.S. is not as bad as many like to believe. We lost the passenger pigeon and no one is quite sure why. We lost the heath hen and the Carolina parakeet. The great auk is gone. Except for the passenger pigeon we hardly miss them, and we've brought in pheasants, chukars, and Hungarian partridge to replace them. Antelope were killed off down to a few thousand. Now they are running around the Southwest like jackrabbits. We have buffalo to spare, and with the great plains fenced in and farmed we have no place to put our excess. It is consistent for us to exploit the natural things we value until they are almost gone, then when the stocks are low and less valuable to exploit and the general population has finally realized that the dollars for a few are robbing them of something to be cherished nationally, they protect them on a gamefish or songbird basis and secure them for all time.

The reason for the salmon's decline is simple. We did not protect the redds or allow enough salmon to reach them and spawn. We did it with a complex system of nets and dams and anglers' flies, with pollution, with rules like placing the saving of mergansers and cormorants above the saving of the salmon and with a commercial net-mesh size forced by law that killed off the best of the breeding stock.

Now we have passed the turning point and are on the long road back. Again, it is just as simple. We must put a full complement of salmon back on the spawning redds. Not just enough salmon to utilize those redds, but, as Darwin would want, enough to compete and to keep the species at its best, adapting and improving, not just staying static. To do that some salmon that do not have the best survival traits for their immediate needs will fail to survive and those with superior endowment will find the best place in nature's balance. The salmon resource will be as simple or as complex to restore as it was to destroy. It will take the same thought and energy on our parts to rebuild it that it took the commercial fishermen to destroy it.

These are the basic things we must do: First, we must reduce the killing of salmon until the stocks are in prime shape. The greatest killers, of course, are the commercial netters who have traditionally taken about eighty-five percent and the very best of the total stocks. How are we doing on that score? Not very well. We've eliminated commercial netting in some of the provinces, but Newfoundland, which has traditionally taken the lion's share, is still taking its heavy toll. Why is this allowed? Consensus is that the people of Newfoundland are poor and need all the money and food that they can get. That is a kind and sentimental excuse but not a good one since, having depleted their own rivers, their major take is of salmon that have been created by conservation measures in and at the cost of other provinces. If poverty is the reason, it is pertinent to ask whether the salmon money goes to the truly poor or to those who are at least moderately wealthy and who have other sources of income.

The Atlantic Salmon Federation had a study made of the salmon's value to Canada. It shows the value of an angling-caught salmon to be about forty times greater in dollars to the economy as one caught commercially, to say nothing of the recreational value to the country. It showed the commercial catch, approximately eighty-five percent of the total, to be worth only about $7 million while the angling catch, about fifteen percent, to be worth $43 million. These are our own figures. They show that making salmon an angling-only fish will benefit Canada greatly. Once this is established, it becomes a certainty that if the anglers can adequately crop the salmon it will eventually become designated as an angling-only fish. On the basis of this truth, it is time to take appropriate action. It is far better to pay subsistence to any poor and deserving people in order to help them survive than to diminish the salmon resource at great cost to the nation.

Some commercial fishermen have claimed that in spite of the cold, hard work of netting, they love it just as much as any angler loves his sport and therefore should be allowed to continue. That is reasonable if they are content to work under the same strict conservation rules and limits that anglers do. If it means continuing to take the great numbers of the best fish—a prospect that has brought us to the present crisis—then it's a poor proposition.

The major fault in the taking of salmon may have been the killing of the largest and best breeding stock of the species in the nets. Through pressure from commercial fishermen, Canadian law has, for well over half a century, dictated a mesh size that would catch the big salmon, the best breeders, while allowing the runts to slip through the gill nets to breed the stock of the future. Because of this policy and this law, rivers that once ran almost all large salmon were converted to rivers with runs composed almost entirely of grilse. It is to counteract this unfortunate policy that anglers on most of our continent's rivers are returning all their large salmon, uninjured, to go on to spawn and rebuild the average size of the runs.

What should be done, in all fairness, is to limit commercial fishermen, like the anglers, to the smaller fish. That can be done by reducing the legal mesh size to, let us say, between three and four inches from the present six, letting the big fish return to their rivers of origin and rebuild their stocks. (Big salmon can safely back out of a net with a mesh too small to catch their gills.) To simply put, let us say, a ninety percent quota on Newfoundland's overall take means that only a very few of the really large fish will be allowed to escape along with most of the ten percent that will be made up of the medium and lesser fish that would be saved. It is only logical and fair that if anglers are forced to put back all or almost all of the big breeding stock they catch then the commercial netters who caused the problem in the first place should make a similar sacrifice to save the salmon. I'm sure the general public, the voting public, would see this as eminently fair and give full support to such a measure. We should put on a crusade for such a ruling and make it a step on the way to gamefish status.

It is reasonable to believe, and biologists agree, that the harvesting of salmon should be controlled, river by river, for the best management. Then those rivers that are in good shape can be harvested to a proper degree and those that are in poor shape can be protected and restored. The taking of salmon indiscriminately in the sea means that salmon from depleted rivers will be taken inadvertently instead of taking only salmon from rivers in good shape. This concept should apply whether the fish are still taken in part commercially or only by angling. Quebec has pointed the way by allowing a larger limit on its rivers in the best shape. The taking of fish only at their native rivers is a natural step on the way to gamefish status.

Fortunately the production of salmon by fish farming makes their flesh available for food for everyone, and the criticism that if salmon were to be made a gamefish then only anglers or the friends they give them to could eat salmon isn't valid. The gamefish designation would have definite advantages. It would mean that all salmon taken would be taken in a manner to give the greatest return economically (through tourism, tackle, guiding, etc.). It would mean that when the salmon runs return to near normal there would not be any way to regress toward the commercial fishery that caused the problem originally. The public in general would welcome any expansion of its salmon angling opportunity.

Our problems have always been overwhelmingly political in nature. Politicians determine who can take what of a publicly owned resource. They are subject to lobbying and payoffs from those who make money in the harvests, and their lobbying influence can only be counteracted by an aroused public. The public and we, the anglers, are not well organized, and because it is not our livelihood as it is for the spoilers, we find neither the time nor the money to compete for political favor in regulations. The unifying of the anglers and organizing the voting power of the public is essential for the force needed to move politicians who bow, quite naturally, to campaign help and, ultimately, to votes.

"Make the Atlantic salmon a gamefish!" will be a rallying cry to unite Canadian anglers from coast to coast, but a simple statement that we'd like to *have the net take reduced* will not draw the same response from our friends the non-salmon anglers and their friends. Those who oppose making the wild Atlantic salmon a gamefish are saying, "Don't make waves." They should know that there is no way to take something valuable away from any group without making waves and creating resentment. It is part of the struggle. If the cause is honorable and the best course for society, then the making of those waves is a worthwhile necessity rather than something to be avoided.

Why doesn't ASF ask for gamefish status for the salmon? Do we not believe that it is best for both the salmon and the Canadian society? Are we, like hesitant youngsters, unsure of ourselves or our purpose? If making the salmon a gamefish is the best thing for our kids and their kids, then it is the thing to do, and if we don't ask for it the political bodies in control will not make it happen. Bargaining is bargaining, and the rule is to ask for what is wanted even though it may not be granted immediately. Salmon as a gamefish will be secure for the foreseeable future. As it is now, it will be subject to repeated attempts to expand the devastation of netting as long as any commercial nets remain legally set. There was an instance where the net berths on a river were brought up only to have the government reissue new net berths in between the old ones, negating the effort and money expended to bring the run of that river back.

Opponents of gamefish classification say that because of the large Newfoundland take it would cost hundreds of millions of dollars to buy out the nets. They say it would upset the people with whom we have been dealing, and they question its constitutionality. Let's take a look.

It is true that the Newfoundland salmon catch is a very large and valuable one. But it is true that it is also mainly a catch of intercepted fish, a catch of matured fry or smolts that were created and paid for by hatcheries and conservation measures at very considerable costs by the provinces of Quebec, New Brunswick and Nova Scotia and by the United States. According to the rules of the sea, these fish belong to the rivers of their origin. They are being stolen on their way home. While this has been going on for a long time, so did slavery. Both are wrong and, just as with slavery, the wrong will be righted, in this case by pressure from the other provinces and the U.S. and from us as well. When that happens, and it will, the Newfoundland netters will have only the runs of their own depleted streams to net, and the cost of buying out the net berths will be peanuts as compared to the present cost. The Newfoundland anglers will then have more public pressure than the commercial fishermen and will support gamefish status.

As to support in Newfoundland, we know it is there. We can all remember that a few years back after the conclave in that province when some of us gave interviews, there was an editorial written in the province's leading newspaper that, among other things, suggested gamefish status as an option. For that article, the writer of the editorial and the publisher were given the ASF's Happy Fraser Award.

Opponents say, too, that nowhere else has the Atlantic salmon been made a gamefish. Therefore, we should not work for it. Are we followers or leaders? We have the facts we need, and I hold that our mandate is to be leaders rather than followers.

As to upsetting our political friends (our commercial enemies are already upset with us), I've talked to some who simply say, "If that's what you want and believe should happen why don't you say so?" What dreadful thing would happen if, now that we have the figures on the comparative economic value of fish caught by angling versus commercial nets or traps, we take the logical gamefish stand? Will those in power say they're going to increase the netting? Cut the number of tags allowed to anglers? Allow the Indian bands to take more fish? We have made the present modest gains in conserving the salmon because of public interest and pressure we have developed. An appeal for gamefish status will not lessen that pressure nor will it create powerful opponents we do not already have. But it will help unite the great majority of anglers in our cause.

Salmon anglers should know that the redfish, a saltwater fish of southeastern United States, whose poundage far exceeds that of the Atlantic salmon, has been made a gamefish in Texas and is about to be made a gamefish throughout its range from that state to North Carolina. The snook, another saltwater commercial fish, has been a gamefish in Florida for many years. These designations as gamefish were not generous gifts from the political entities that controlled them but were the result of dedicated efforts by anglers.

As to the constitutionality of such a move, I find it hard to see where the passage of a law designating the wild Atlantic salmon as a gamefish, a fish for which there would be no commercial catch or sale, is in conflict with the constitution any more than eliminating the sale of elk, mountain sheep or deer is. Gamefish status would allow, as in the U.S., the taking of fish and game by native Indians on their reservations for food but not commercial sale.

The establishment of our Atlantic salmon as a gamefish will secure it for all time with its maximum benefit financially and recreationally for Canada. No one should doubt that our aim is to achieve what is best for the country as a whole. With that final goal in mind the steps toward achievement will fall into place more logically and more swiftly than will piecemeal efforts. The time is now.

[1990]

CHAPTER TWENTY-SEVEN

TERRESTRIALS FOR SALMON

*I*t's always a wonderful thing for an inventive fisherman when the implementation of an idea turns into better fishing along the river. Fly patterns imitative of terrestrial insects are just this side of heresy in salmon fishing, but they work. A salmon-fly ant or moth doesn't have the classical cachet of a Jock Scott or Silver Doctor, but for the ever-pragmatic Lee Wulff they were yet another window into the world of Atlantic salmon.

· · · · · · · · ·

THE BIOLOGISTS TELL US that the Atlantic salmon *cannot digest food* when it returns to the fresh water of its native river. Yet, paradoxically, it does rise, on occasion, to take a food imitation in its mouth. On that slim whim of the salmon we base our angling efforts.

Sometimes I hear salmon fishermen say with surprise that they actually saw a salmon rising to a mayfly or other natural insect as it drifted down over its lie. That shouldn't be surprising. If we do our best to imitate natural insects with our artificial creations, why should we not expect salmon to rise occasionally to the real thing?

We can believe that the main reason for the Atlantic salmon's rising to our flies is from a memory of its almost entirely insectivorous feeding during its parr life. This memory pattern is demonstrated by the fact that the grilse, only one year away from the parr feeding, rise much more readily than the larger fish that are two years or more away from those memories. In contrast, the Pacific salmon, which have a relatively short parr life and feed more on plankton than on insects, do not rise well to our traditional salmon flies, which are insect imitations.

If, then, the insects of parr life are the most logical things for an angler to imitate, why have we been so slow in imitating some of the best naturals to be found in the salmon streams? I believe it is because of the way our flies have followed the fashions originated in our salmon angling's British beginnings rather than simple logic. For hundreds of years we swam *winged* insect imitations *underwater* where no winged insect ever expected to be and no salmon or parr ever expected to see one, even though we knew the nymphs or underwater forms of the insects had no wings. We made our wet flies with wings, hackles (legs), body and tail. Not till Skues and Hewitt made us feel ridiculous did we use nymphs at all. We did let hundreds of old trout patterns like the Greenwell's Glory and Wickham's Fancy fade into oblivion but we kept all the tried and true salmon patterns like the Jock Scott, Dusty Miller, Green Highlander and the rest. We felt they were beautiful to use and we knew they worked. We did not realize that they worked more because of their motion than because of their special designs. Every parr learns in early life that when he takes all the drifting things that come by he gets a lot of wood and nonedible material but that if he concentrates on those things that move through the water rather than drift with it he gets a lot of nourishment. He learns to seek out those things which show movement and life. It may either be movement through the water or movement within the fly. The movement of hackles is like the breathing of the gills of a mayfly nymph.

Terrestrials are a part of the parr's stream feeding. It should not be surprising that my best fly two summers ago was a carpenter ant, big and black and on a #6 hook. A good salmon on the Hunt rose to it after refusing a few of my favorites. Later, on the Grand Cascapedia's Big Curly Pool, two salmon rose deliberately through the clear slowly twisting water to take that drifting ant. Still later, on the Upsalquitch, my friend Bruce Waterfall took his only big salmon of the trip on the drifting carpenter. With all the ants that abound in salmondom, why didn't we have an ant pattern long ago?

Last year at Mrs. Guest's Pool on the Grand Cascapedia two salmon rose savagely to take an imitation dragonfly. On the Upsalquitch I caught one on a flat floating delta-winged moth imitation like the many moths that abound in the woods and may be as common in the air over them as mayflies are.

Can it be that we salmon anglers have too long been blind to the importance of terrestrials in the diet of the parr and too long tied to the conventions of the fly patterns of yesterday? I view those old patterns as great works of art and ingenuity, but I have to ask whether a grasshopper imitation might not work as well as a Bomber if it, too, floats half drowned in the surface film. Is there a special moth that the parr of your river like above all other insects? Will an ant catch salmon for you that a Silver Doctor will not? It should be interesting to find out.

[1985]

CHAPTER TWENTY-EIGHT

THE "RIVVELING" HITCH

*T*he riffling hitch is a special wet-fly method that causes
the fly to swim along the water's surface, making a small V-wake
as it passes near the fish. Salmon sometimes find this irresistible,
as Wulff discovered back in the 1940s when he first brought this
technique to the attention of the angling world. He recounts the
discovery and the method in this 1987 chapter, to which I'll add
as a footnote that many northwestern anglers have found the
method to be equally effective for steelhead.

ONE OF THE MAJOR CHANGES in salmon fly fishing in this century
has been the use of the Portland Creek Hitch. It is called by

many names but I use "Portland Creek" because that's where it originated. It may be good here to give a short history of this unique fishing technique.

The story begins with the old-style flies. Until about 1920 flies were tied on snelled hooks. They were not eyed, and the silkworm gut, or snell, was wrapped to the straight shank with thread and then varnished, and the fly was fashioned on the hook with the gut strands attached. Trout flies were tied to a snell about five inches long. The gut strand was doubled with a loop at the end, which was locked into a loop on the leader. Most leaders were made in six-foot lengths with three loops for attaching flies and one at the end to be tied to the line. Salmon flies were tied with a very short loop of doubled gut, which was looped (or tied) directly to the leader.

Then eyed hooks for flies were developed, and they replaced snelled hooks. The snelled ones were no longer made, but some fishermen continued to use them. One of their difficulties was that after a few years the gut rotted or became brittle and weak, and most fishermen quit using them for fear they'd break when a fish was hooked. This was particularly true of salmon fishermen, who needed stronger leaders to put considerable playing strain on their fish.

The British Navy covered the world, and wherever there was fly fishing the men, particularly the officers, often fished. When they charted the coast of Newfoundland they went ashore to fish and, of course, they found the best fishing in the out-of-the-way places where the settlements were small or there were no settlers at all. Portland Creek was a river with no settlement on it and only a small village nearby, and the Navy fished there.

The officers had a habit of giving flies to the local people who showed them the rivers and, more often than not, they gave away the beautiful but obsolete flies with weakened gut eyes. Of course when the locals fished with them they lost salmon after salmon. Of all other salmon rivers of the world where British officers fished, those who received the gut-eyed flies simply cursed the Royal Navy, but at Portland Creek some angry but inventive individual not only tied his leader to the gut eye but also took two half-hitches behind the head of the fly to make sure no salmon could break away.

On no other river in the world would a fly attached that easy have been so successful. Those who fished Portland Creek for salmon with their flies tied that way caught far more salmon than they had ever been able to catch before. They found too that they lost no greater percentage of fish on hitched flies than they did with flies they tied on conventionally.

When I first went to Portland Creek and was told that if I wanted to catch salmon I'd have to "hitch" my fly, I didn't believe it. I fished for hours in the conventional way with wet flies and didn't have a rise. Then a strong wind came up and kept my line and leader on the surface instead of under it. Twice a salmon made a pass at one of the leader knots that was skimming the surface and making a small V-wake. I then put two half-hitches behind the head of the fly I'd been fishing with and let it skim across the top. The first cast brought a strike from the salmon, and he was hooked and landed.

To hitch a fly, it's tied to the leader in the normal way with whatever knot one chooses, and then two half-hitches of the leader are tied just behind the fly head. With a double hook the leader should come off in the center of the throat of the fly, and with a single hook it should come off on the side that will make the fly skim the surface with the point of the hook downstream. The simple rule is that if the stream is flowing away to your left, the leader should come off the fly's left side; if it flows to the right, the leader should come off the right side. After a cast the line must be tightened to keep the fly on the surface. If it sinks it may not rise to the surface but stay underneath, twisting, which doesn't seem to catch salmon. On a normal retrieve, the speed of the current keeps the fly skimming along the path a conventional wet fly would take under water, letting the angler see his fly and know where it is at all times. If a fish moves beneath it he's more likely to see the motion and concentrate on that spot.

If the fly moves too slowly and threatens to sink, as in a slow flow, the angler can lift his rod or take in line to bring it up to speed. If it moves too swiftly and bounces or bubbles on the surface, lowering the rod can slow it down. A fly can be hitched and will skim with a sunken leader when using an intermediate line. There seems to be a perfect speed of movement that experienced anglers try to achieve.

Over the many years I fished Portland Creek I ran occasional tests, fishing a wet fly conventionally, under the surface, and then, for the same amount of time, with the hitch, skimming the surface. The hitched fly was about twenty times as effective. That was strange because only eighteen miles away, on the River of Ponds, my testing showed the effectiveness of both methods to be about the same. I've fished many rivers around the North Atlantic, and on no other river has the hitched fly proven to be so much more effective than a conventional wet.

The local fisherman at Portland Creek (and there were only a very few of them when I first fished there) were of west of England stock. Their living was primitive by our standards—they knew boats and dogsleds but had never seen a train, an automobile or an airplane. They spoke with an accent like the people of the Outer Banks of North Carolina. A fir tree was a "var," a dredge was a "drudge." They added an "h" before words starting with vowels and dropped the "h" on words starting with that sound. An eagle was a "heagle" and a horse was a " 'orse." To them it was the "rivvling" (riffling) hitch and so we called it at my fishing camps on that river. Worldwide it may be called the Newfoundland Hitch or by some other name, but most often just a hitch.

I brought it to the attention of fishermen in a story in *Outdoor Life* in 1946, and since then it has spread slowly and is still spreading throughout the angling world.

In 1962, when I was in Britain and fished on the Scottish Dee with my six-foot fly rod against "Jock Scott" and his sixteen-footer, I showed the hitch and caught salmon, although the British anglers I spoke with swore no salmon would take such a crazy-acting fly. In Iceland the hitch seems to work at least as well as, and probably better than, the conventionally fished wet fly. Apparently the word has not spread very far. I was back in Scotland two years ago, and none of the anglers I spoke to on the Spey knew of it or fished that way, ever.

As a result of my *Outdoor Life* story Bill Nelson and a group of anglers he fished with decided to try the hitch on steelhead in our western streams. It worked very well and they kept it a secret for some time before the word got out. Now it is an accepted way to fish for steelhead.

I've fished for trout with it, using small flies and fine leaders, and caught some difficult fish. Some day it may be a recognized trout technique, too. The hitch has caught a lot of fish for a lot of anglers, and it has given me success on rivers where other methods have failed. And I was able to give something back to the anglers of Portland Creek who gave me the hitch. I brought them the dry fly, which they'd never seen or used before, and the dry is just as effective on Portland Creek salmon as the hitch is.

[1987]

CHAPTER TWENTY-NINE

LUCKY OR SMART?

Luck—or chance, if you will—is what makes angling a sport. If every element of fishing were predictable, it would become an operation by rote and very little fun. Fishing, too, is a great leveler; a fish, after all, has no idea who's holding the fishing rod. Other things being equal, a banker and a beggar have the same chance of hooking a fish. Fishing is such a broad arena of chance and skill that no fisherman, regardless of skill, is immune from the effects of pure chance. Why, even when I went fishing with Lee Wulff, I wished him good luck!

- - - - - - - - -

ONE OF THE THINGS that comes up frequently in angling discussions is the question of luck. How important is luck in a given situation? In what situations is luck most important?

Luck seems to be the most important where big fish are concerned. The capture of an exceptionally large fish is, more often than not, a matter of luck. Because of some special circumstances a particular fish grows much larger than most others of its species. Where it swims and whose fly it happens to come upon and decides to take is, without question, mostly luck, at least where the fish has lots of water to move around in. It becomes less true where the fish takes up a lie, as a big trout might in a particular part of a certain pool. Then, when a good many anglers know about the fish and all try to catch him, there's a little luck in finding that fish in a taking mood. And the capture is much more dependent on the skill of the presentation and the playing.

Luck can be a wonderful thing when a parent takes a youngster fishing with bait, where presentation is least important. There the biggest fish, the prize of the day, is as likely to be caught by an inexperienced angler as an old pro. If fishing always required great skill, like golf, it would be much more difficult to bring new recruits into the fold or to give them the basics of understanding how fish feed and what their instincts and reactions are.

Technological advances have taken a lot of the luck out of some types of fishing. In my youth, when we trolled the lakes for fish that might be well below the surface, it was necessary to learn where the ledges and drop-offs were. Through getting hung up, or taking soundings with the anchors, or just remembering where fish were caught and at what depths, we learned the topography of the lakebeds. We located those good spots by sighting along prominent points on the shore to get crossing lines to fix our position. It took a lot of time to learn a lake and a lot of experience to know just where to fish or how to troll a particular bait. Now, with depth sounders we can discover the bathymetry of a lake in no time at all. We can even get a sounder that actually shows us fish beneath us on our screen and, with a little experience, their size and species. Fishing the deeper lakes has changed from being luck to largely a matter of equipment and the information it gives. In the ocean too, with temperature and depth readings, we can narrow down the best fishing areas, big as they are. But if two similar boats fish similar lures in a similar fashion in a particular ocean area, one may strike fish while the other is blanked. Most ocean fish have not been fished over much and they strike readily; finding them is usually more important than making a perfect presentation, and luck is a major factor.

It's easy to find fish in streams. They're never deeper than the deepest pool and they're limited to water suitable for their feeding, safety and comfort. But in streams, where fish are easier to find, they become harder and harder to fool and the presentation becomes increasingly important.

Luck depends a great deal on weather and water conditions. Luck gives you a shower that puts the trout in a feeding mood because of all the terrestrial food washing into the stream. Bad luck puts the water temperature of a stream up in the seventies, driving the fish to leave that stretch barren and go to the cooler spring holes or tributaries. Skill is the angler's knowing where those are.

Failing to understand the nature of what you fish for can give a false impression of an angler's luck. Atlantic salmon fishing, to most trout fishermen, seems a matter of luck because the salmon is an unusual fish. Since it is not fished for during its stream life as a parr or in its long sea journey, it is unsophisticated as far as flies and lures go. If it were a normal predator it would be easy to catch on a piece of bacon or almost anything edible passed in front of it. But because nature takes away its ability to digest food when it returns to fresh water (lest it eat up all the young salmon and destroy its own species), it rises only on a whim and, unless one fishes with a certain type of fly in a certain manner, one is not likely to catch a salmon. The particular fly presentation that will put a salmon into the mood to take it is an uncertain thing; they do strange things because of it.

Atlantic salmon have been known to take a fly eagerly when it was thrown into the water right beside the canoe preparatory to making the first cast. Yet some are completely resistent to flies no matter how skillful the angler because they have no real need or interest in food. Their strange behavior makes most trout fishermen who come to fish for salmon think it's "chuck it and chance it," and what they see seems to confirm it. However, when I ran a salmon camp I knew which guides would have their sportsmen catch the most fish. Year after year it was the guides who understood the fish and put their charges in those spots with those flies and with those casts for the best chance of success.

I once took a good friend who was a fine trout fisherman to a remote Labrador pool in my seaplane. The river split around a rocky ledge to make two entries into a big pool. I gave him an outfit identical to mine. I put him on the side of the larger and better of the two flows while I fished the lesser one. On the first cast I hooked a small salmon and landed it. A few casts later brought in another. I could see my friend was upset.

"Why don't you take this place," I suggested.

We changed places and I began catching salmon where he had been while he didn't raise a fish. Finally he came over and said, "You must be doing something that I'm not. What is it?"

I explained, as best I could, that I believed a certain speed or retrieve, with the fly dead crosswise to the current, seemed to work better than random casts—but that a salmon might take a fly no matter how it was presented. He watched me and finally said, "I can do that."

With a little bit of change in his normal wet-fly casting he too began catching salmon. Small differences in fishing techniques that the uninitiated may think to be the result of luck often are not.

There are times when your ego tells you you've just been unlucky. Take last summer on the Upsalquitch: In our week of fishing only twelve salmon were taken. Some by my daughter-in-law, Ginger, who had far less fishing experience than the rest of us. She fished simply and conventionally. On a day when we fished from the same canoe, I suggested she take the first drop, which she did.

She hooked and landed a fish. I fished the next drop carefully and had not a rise. On the next drop she hooked and landed another fish. From then on throughout the pool and during the whole afternoon neither of us had another rise from a salmon.

It is comforting to say that all week long the "taking" fish just happened to be in the water allotted to her. But nine for her and only three for the five of us old-timers seems to be stretching the power of coincidence. Or was it?

The most difficult example to explain happened many years ago on New York's Saratoga Lake. I'd taken a relative who didn't fish but wanted to learn about baitcasting for the bass, pike and walleyes. After a bit of instruction he could cast well enough to fish. We fished all afternoon and I wanted badly for him to like fishing and become a pleasant companion for future days. But Willie never had a strike while I caught eighteen fish by the end of the afternoon. If I caught a fish on a certain plug or spoon I immediately turned my rod over to Willie and fished with his. We must have changed rods a couple dozen times, and to this day I can't explain it. Was it just that I had a different retrieve and that made all the difference, as with the salmon in the Labrador pool? That's hard to believe because we were using plugs and wobbling spoons that had their own actions. How could any little idiosyncrasy of mine have made such a devastating difference? Willie was about thirty-five and I don't believe he ever fished again, even though his brother had a camp on the lake. Was it pure coincidence? As on the Upsalquitch, that is hard to believe. I will continue to try to be the best, the wisest fisherman I possibly can, but no matter how you slice it, I like to believe that it is better to be lucky than smart.

[1991]

CHAPTER THIRTY

OVER THE YEARS

*I*n this last chapter, Wulff looked back at some of the major changes he saw in a long lifetime of angling. At the time of his death, he was still chasing salmon in summer, bonefish in the winter, and trout and other fish in-between. To the end, he was a fountain of new angling ideas, and like many readers I'll miss his voice.

ONE OF THE GREAT BOONS in modern angling was the introduction of nylon for leaders. Before that time (1940, I believe), we had to use silkworm gut, the stretched-out gob of material the worm was going to make into silk. It came in lengths of from nine to sixteen inches, depending on the diameter. That meant a lot of knots in every leader. Silkworm gut, to be tied in a knot or made ready for use, had to be soaked in pads dampened with water or glycerine or a combination of both. Nylon filament, long and strong, solved a major fishing problem of the past.

It also made a change in my personal appearance on the rivers, because in order to carry leaders all tied up and ready to fish, I carried a couple wrapped around the band of my hat. In coils of that diameter, silkworm gut straightened well enough to be fished without soaking. With nylon I didn't need the hat. I figured if people could go bareheaded before we had hats and dark glasses, I could do it too. And so I did. Only with receding eye capability in my seventies did I go back to wearing a hat and dark glasses.

The flies of the early thirties were traditional wet flies. I used to give White Wulffs to friendly fishermen I met on the rivers. I'd meet them again the following year and find those dry flies still in their boxes, unused. They just didn't look like salmon flies should to those anglers, and they had no faith in them. Faith was slow in coming, but the few of us who used dry flies then were so successful that conversions took place and, eventually, acceptance came.

After the Second World War, when many trout fishermen came to the salmon rivers with trout flies but few typical salmon patterns, they tried their trout flies on the salmon and had considerable success. Flies like the Muddler (1950) proved successful and patterns like the Surface Stonefly (1950) and the Bomber (1960s), which floated in the surface film, became deadly on the salmon pools. The great variety of shapes and sizes in flies that a salmon would take surprised the old-time salmon anglers.

A few years ago, when I caught salmon on flies that imitated an ant and a dragonfly, it was the first time, to my knowledge, that terrestrial patterns were made up as salmon patterns. Why did we wait so long? If we made flies to imitate aquatic insects because parr ate them and had long memories, as many salmon fishermen believe, why not terrestrials which parr are also known to feed on? Our minds have been opening to realities rather than being constrained to the hallowed patterns of custom.

There were also major changes in rod materials. When I started salmon fishing, they were basically bamboo with a lesser percentage of solid woods like greenheart of lancewood. The length of the rods in use was usually thirteen feet or better. Tonkin cane, a superior bamboo, was introduced. Rod materials then made several jumps. On the old bamboo rods, the varnish would crack at the metal ferrules because the wood bent and the steel did not. If they were fished in rain and not dried out religiously afterward, the wood at the ferrules would weaken due to moisture-softening and would eventually break. The first answer to that was Bakelite impregnation, developed by Fred Longacre, which made the bamboo impervious to water and dampness. The next was the coming of glass fibers, developed by Dr. Howald, which were as strong, more flexible, and also impervious to water.

At first the glass rods were made with steel ferrules, which still gave a dead spot. Then self-ferrules were developed which gave bending within the ferrules. And finally graphite and boron came on the scene. They were lighter and stronger materials with great moduli of elasticity. They made fly-fishing a lot less work and attracted more people to the sport.

Fly lines changed, too, both in design and composition. Until the fifties, they were made of silk and coated or saturated with linseed oil or some other preparation. They were slightly heavier than water and sank, but sank slowly. That meant an angler's flies stayed on or near the surface. Essentially, an Atlantic salmon always had to leave his lie, and rise to or almost to the surface to take a fly. This was good. Provincial laws stipulated unweighted flies and "surface fly fishing" as the only legal method of taking salmon.

In Europe, salmon fishing was private and a riparian owner could have his guests or himself fish with any tackle he wished, constantly having in mind the quality of the fishing he owned lest it deteriorate. On this side of the Atlantic, with most of the fishing public, it was deemed necessary to eliminate lures and weighted flies, or anything else that would let a fisherman get his hook or hooks down to the level where salmon are. Therefore, any weight on fly, leader or line, and the use of treble hooks, was barred to protect the salmon.

Given weight and double or treble hooks, a "jigger" can foul-hook salmon with ease. I grew up in Alaska at a time when the foul-hooking, spearing, snaring and gaffing of fish was legal. The best jiggers could snag fish they couldn't even see because of cloudy water. They simply knew where the trout or salmon should be lying and let their hooks drift into the right places for the snatch, losing a few trebles or weights to the rocks but taking a great many fish.

With the changes in fly-line manufacture in the fifties came sinking lines. Our laws were not updated to specifically outlaw those lines beyond the "intermediate" category, equivalent to the specific gravity of the old silk ones. Many trout fishermen, who had become used to sinking lines and heavy sink tips in that type of fishing, assumed it was okay to fish on the salmon streams with sinking lines and proceeded to do so. Most of them weren't interested in snagging fish, but some were.

Foul-hooking fish demonstrates a breakdown in the sporting ethic. It negates everything most anglers hold honorable. I think it is time to eliminate fishing salmon lines with a specific gravity greater than 1.20, and to outlaw weighted flies, as well. Even if an angler with fast-sinking line does not foul-hook a fish, he becomes more deadly because he fishes at the salmon's level— and a salmon, having no hands to feel things with, will often take a fly into his mouth just out of curiosity.

Anglers are always trying to find more successful ways of catching fish. Every time they do, they cause more fish to be taken from the rivers (except under catch-and-release), which means that to maintain the salmon runs at the previous level, either the season would have to be shortened or the limit lowered. This is something not all fishermen realize. The more fish there are in the stream, the better the fishing. A stream that is barren of fish gives sport to no one. Making salmon fishing easier dilutes the sport.

Quebec now allows the use of treble hooks up to #6. This is to allow the use of tube flies, which are commonly used in Europe with a treble hook rather than a single or double. I think the sport has lost some of its dignity and quality with this move. First, a #6 hook is a capable jigging hook. Second, it is a move to increase the catching of fish which, as just explained, is not a move toward conservation.

Salmon fishing, with its present difficulty factor, is an excellent sport. A tube fly lacks the dignity of traditional flies, as it has no top or bottom and may ride in the water at any angle. It may be a good imitation of an elver, but it could be just as effective as other flies if limited to a conventional hook. Its users would no longer have a special advantage over those using conventional flies.

Double hooks are not necessary to catch salmon, as all dry-fly fishermen consistently prove. Are wet-fly fishermen such inferior players of salmon that they cannot land their fish on a single hook?

The presently legal double hooks make it very easy for a fisherman to foul-hook salmon. They are heavy, and if cast upstream with slack, will often sink to the fish's level. Being doubles, they will foul-hook a fish far more readily than a single. A great many salmon that have been foul-hooked this way, with legal tackle, could have been saved for spawning or for a true sportsman if a single-hook-only law were on the books and enforced.

The other basic line change, that of design, brought in the forward taper. This concentration of weight at the forward end of the lines gave greater distance and let shorter rods, in the nine- or nine-and-a-half-foot range, cast far enough to replace almost all the longer rods. Rods became easier to carry and less tiring to use.

It was easy to see where salmon fishing was headed back in the midthirties, and I began releasing fish, writing and making films to extol the benefits of catch-and-release. Those efforts were met with ridicule and scorn.

The change was slow in coming. Nova Scotia was the first province to officially recognize catch-and-release, with special regulations to restore the spring run of big fish in the Margaree. It pleases me to have lived long enough to see catch-and-release accepted as a valuable conservation tool and its use widespread enough to build back our stocks and give pleasure to many more fishermen.

[1988]

INDEX

About the Author

Lee Wulff was born in Valdez, Alaska, in 1905, and was graduated from Stanford University with a civil-engineering degree. Before becoming a freelance artist and writer and, eventually, a film producer, he studied art in Paris and was an art director for a New York advertising agency. His outdoor films were first to be featured on network television (CBS), and he spent ten years as a producer for ABC's *American Sportsman* television series. He was a regular columnist for *Fly Rod & Reel* magazine. A longtime advocate of fisheries conservation and the environment, he served as an officer and director of The Atlantic Salmon Federation. *Salmon on a Fly* is his eighth angling book. Lee Wulff died in a plane crash on April 28, 1991.

About the Editor

John Merwin was for several years an editor of *Fly Fisherman* magazine, the largest special-interest magazine in this field. He was also the founding editor and publisher of *Fly Rod & Reel* (a consumer magazine) and *Fly Tackle Dealer* (the industry's only trade magazine). He spent five years as the executive director of The American Museum of Fly Fishing, which has become world-famous for its collections, exhibits and research activities pertaining to fly fishing. He is the author and/or editor of eleven angling books and was a contributor to three major anthologies on the same topic.